DATE DUE

NOT TO WORRY!

NOT TO WORRY!

HOW TO FREE YOURSELF FROM
UNNECESSARY ANXIETY AND
CHANNEL YOUR WORRIES
INTO POSITIVE ACTION

MARY McCLURE GOULDING, M.S.W.
ROBERT L. GOULDING, M.D.

INCLUDES A TESTED 6 — DAY
PROGRAM FOR "LETTING GO"

Silver Arrow Books
William Morrow

Library of Congress Cataloging-in-Publication Data

Goulding, Mary McClure, 1925–
Not to worry! : how to free yourself from unnecessary anxiety and
channel your worries into positive action / Mary McClure Goulding,
Robert L. Goulding.
p.   cm.
"Includes a tested 6-day program for 'letting go.'"
Includes index.
ISBN 0-688-08480-X
1. Worry.   2. Happiness.   I. Goulding, Robert L., 1917–
II. Title.
BF575.W8G6   1989
158'.1—dc19   88-13866
CIP

Printed in the United States of America

First Edition

1 2 3 4 5 6 7 8 9 10

BOOK DESIGN BY JAYE ZIMET

TO GLORIA

Thanks to:

Joan Minninger, Ph.D., for encouraging us to write about worrying.

Michael F. Hoyt, Ph.D., Robert L. Bettinger, Ph.D., and Jeanne Leventhal, M.D., for reading the first draft and offering excellent suggestions.

Muriel James, Ed.D., for her self-parenting concepts in her many books.

Karen Edwards, Chris Butler, Claudia Edwards Pagano, David Edwards, M.A., and Carol Edwards for care, inspiration, and for both interesting worries and antiworry one-liners.

Bernie Mazel, for starting us on our writing careers and for finding us Sherry Arden and Jennifer Williams.

CONTENTS

PART I

PART II

PART III

PART IV

PART I

CHAPTER 1

THE WORRY ADDICTION

Worriers are really nice people. They are the kind of people who pay their taxes, vote in all elections, and put their garbage into secured garbage cans that dogs cannot pry open. They don't carry knives. They try hard to do what is right. Their children are clean and, if they too are worriers, tend to be polite and well-mannered.

Worriers are creative. They can take any small stimulus and weave it into an elaborate fiction. One bounced check can grow into an entire bankruptcy scenario, and one poor report card can become a fantasized failure of epic proportions.

Worriers are more intelligent than average, which can be seen by their quick ability to move from the concrete to the abstract and back, within seconds.

Worriers are sufferers. When people worry, they leave the here-and-now in order to create unpleasant, imaginary stories. During a wonderful meal at a fancy restaurant, they imagine a burglar breaking into their home and stealing everything. During the peaceful moments of the late afternoon before the children have returned from play, they write imaginary horror stories of child abduction. During sex, they think about contraceptive failure.

Worriers are caring people. They will tell you, "If I didn't love you so much, I wouldn't worry about you."

In fact, worriers are exactly the sort of people everyone wants for neighbors, as long as they don't corner you to talk about their worries. The worst fault worriers have is that they tend to be boring. Listening to their worries is about as fascinating as listening to a recital of bowel problems.

Minor worriers may give themselves only a moment of displeasure on an otherwise lovely day. "Oh, dear, what will I do if the bus is late?" After a bit of a stew and a few prognostications of disaster, they'll end up telling themselves, "It doesn't really matter and there's nothing I can do about it anyway." Then they will continue enjoying the brightness of the day and the row of flowering acacias down the street.

For others, worry can be one of the most painful sensations a human being endures. The fact that worry is a self-inflicted torture makes the pain no less real. Worrying causes feelings of fear, shame, and depression. It also causes headaches, insomnia, and can trigger high blood pressure, an asthma attack, or a migraine headache.

John was a worrier about money and security. When he was a child, his parents pointed out to him the old brick building that was the county poorhouse and they told him, over and over again, that he would end up there if he didn't have a secure job and save his money. He'd done what they said and was now postmaster in his small town. He had a good life, with a loving wife, who taught high school English, and two daughters he adored. The day his daughter, Ann, was getting married, he wanted to be happy. Instead, he tortured himself with worry and ended up with a violent headache and nausea. The wedding was a misery for him.

Ann was marrying a nice enough young man, but right after the ceremony they were leaving to go backpacking around the world. John couldn't believe that anyone would be so foolish as to do that before having enough money in the bank to be secure. He kept worrying that they would

turn out to be ne'er-do-wells, who would never have jobs
or be financially independent. The poorhouse, which was
long ago demolished in his county, continued to exist un-
changed in John's mind. The truth is: Ann and her husband
might have any sort of future, happy or sad, rich or poor,
healthy or sick. John couldn't really predict, nor would his
worries change his daughter's life. All that his worries accomplished was to take away his joy during what should
have been for him a very beautiful day.

Worrying can affect a person's love life. When Janet met
Tom, she was sixty years old and had been widowed twice.
Both of her husbands died suddenly of heart attacks. Tom
and Janet discovered they shared many of the same interests,
such as bird-watching, hiking, and reading Shakespeare
aloud. They began a happy friendship that was deepening
into love, when suddenly Janet began to worry. This man
was healthy, just like her previous husbands, but what if he,
too, died of a heart attack? Janet was too intelligent to believe
in magic or a malevolent fate. In no way did she blame
herself for the deaths of her previous husbands. However,
each time she saw Tom, she began to worry that he might
die. To avoid the pain of worrying, she stopped seeing him
and decided she would never again let herself become fond
of a man.

Worries can cause job problems. Dave gave up being a
trial lawyer because of his worries about his performance
in court. Marilyn, when she entered therapy, said her problem was her inability to do well on the job. She soon learned
that her primary problem was obsessive worrying. She had
been a performance worrier since childhood and had believed her worrying made her successful. "If I hadn't worried, I might have goofed off like other kids." After
graduating from college with honors, she was hired by an
engineering firm, and for the first time began to experience
failure. She did twice as much as was wanted or paid for,
just as she had done when she got A's in school, but now
she was told that she wasn't keeping up with her share of

the work load. In effect, they were telling her to stop being compulsive and to turn in her work. Of course, this didn't help. She escalated her worries, becoming frantic that she would fail, and the more she worried, the less she accomplished. She lost her job. Her worries had come true, not in spite of the worries, but because of them.

Even when worry brings tragedy to people's lives, worriers get only limited sympathy from others. At first their friends may sympathize or try to argue them out of their worries, but after a while, the friends laugh at worriers, scold them, or grow bored with their tales of potential doom. Worriers learn to be "closet self-torturers," as they worry in secret. And they begin to worry about worrying, suspecting that their worries prove "there's something wrong with me."

Actually something is wrong. Worriers are addicts. They are addicted to their worries, just as others are addicted to drugs or alcohol. Worry is a self-inflicted, psychological addiction, which people learn in childhood and continue throughout their lives. It is a habit that can put a pall of gloom over hours or days or even a lifetime.

The good news is that this addiction is curable. Even Janet, when she realized that her worry addiction began long before the death of her first husband, was willing to believe that she could be cured. She telephoned Tom and invited him to dinner. After dinner she confessed that she hadn't been seeing him because of her irrational worries about him. She asked if he would be willing to stand by her while she learned to stop worrying. He was delighted, and within less than a month she was no longer plaguing herself with death worries. In fact in that month she gave up her lifelong worry addiction.

John learned to laugh at his poorhouse worries during a five-day workshop for worriers. He was a much freer and happier man when his daughter and son-in-law returned from their travels.

Marilyn used the content of her worries to understand

herself. That is another piece of good news for worry addicts. By examining worries, people can learn much about their own lives and can begin to sort out the ways in which they want to change themselves. Marilyn found that she had focused her life on getting A's in subjects she didn't like and doing jobs that brought her no joy. She also recognized that her kind of worrying and perfectionism was the way she had of avoiding real contact with other people. She is no longer a worry addict, and she is a far richer and more beautiful person than she'd ever have believed possible.

The worrying addiction is curable. In this book you can learn how to use your worries, as Marilyn did, to understand yourself and to solve personal problems. You can teach yourself to be in charge of your own imagination and to use it to serve you rather than to torture you. You can also have a fine time doing this, because learning and doing and changing and having fun go together. You can stop worrying today, tomorrow, or in a week.

CHAPTER 2

LEARNING TO WORRY

Nobody is a born worrier. Worry is a learned response that requires memory, imagination, and a sense of time. A baby will scream in alarm on falling or hearing a loud noise, but hasn't the capacity to turn this into a worry. Later the baby will develop sufficient memory to fear the repetition of an unpleasant event. At that point a child who has had painful experiences in the doctor's office may start to cry on seeing a person wearing a white coat or may fight being carried into the office. Later, with the development of imagination, that child will begin to invent worries about events that have never happened. Remember?

Jean lies as stiff as a stick, not daring to move, with the sheet pulled up over her head. If IT can see her head sticking out from under the sheet, IT will get her! IT is nebulous, face and form unknown, and IT lurks just outside the window, in the closet, or, worst of all, under the bed. If she moves at all, IT will pounce! If only there were no ITs, Jean wouldn't need to cover her whole body and head and even her hair with the hot sheet. She could have the window open and the covers off and feel a breeze, but instead she is terrified and immobilized by her own imagination.

She has to pee. She waits and waits and finally peeks over the edge of the upper sheet, and, yes, the room is still black-dark. There is no light, no sound anywhere, and her need gets worse. She dare not put even one foot outside the covers. IT is now definitely under the bed, waiting to grab her. "Mama, I've got to go to the bathroom!"

Oh, bliss, Mother calls back. "Then go!" She's alive right in the next room.

"I can't! It's dark!"

Oh, what a splendid home, what a fine, wonderful mother. Mother comes in, she's there beside the bed, and instantly there are no ITs . . . until Jean has peed, and Mother has disappeared again, and Jean is stiff with fear in the hot summer darkness.

When the sun comes up, IT vanishes with the dark and Jean is worry-free, until it is bedtime again.

Besides being a self-torturer who invents worries that have never happened and won't happen, Jean also worries about doctors and pain. Like the small child in the doctor's office, she worries in anticipation of events that are, inexorably, going to occur.

One summer Jean's whole family has boils, just like in the Bible, when the Lord punished the Egyptians. It certainly isn't clear what Jean's family is being punished for. Jean's mother says, "You kids brought them home from school." In the past, they had "brought home from school" measles, mumps, chicken pox, scarlet fever, and whooping cough. It's enough to make one wonder if school is worth the infectious dangers lurking there.

There are no antibiotics in these days and therefore no quick cures. Instead, the doctor comes to

their house every afternoon to lance the boils and
to diagnose whether any of them have turned into
carbuncles, which are even worse than boils. Perhaps he makes house calls in order to keep the
infection out of his office, but more probably he
figures that his other sick patients can't tolerate
screaming Jean and her four screaming sisters. Jean
and her four little sisters, tortured with boils and
the doctor, plagued like the Egyptians but certainly
for no good reason, begin to scream as soon as they
see the doctor's car coming up the hill toward their
house. They don't stop screaming until he and his
car are out of sight.

Then the little sisters all stop screaming and
start to play again. They are quite clear about the
periods of pleasure and the periods of torture and
don't allow either to invade the other. Jean worries
all day as she looks for new boils and touches her
tender old ones to determine if they are drying up
or becoming carbuncles.

Some children start worrying at one age, some at
another. Ruth, like Jean, starts young.

She is now five years old, going on six, and she has
been looking forward to first grade for a very long
time, at least half a year. She's exactly two days too
young for first grade by the laws of the state of
California, but her preschool teachers and her
mother decided that Ruth would be ready this year,
so the plans were laid early. Last year Ruth was
enrolled in a private kindergarten in order to qualify. There had been a fair amount of talk at home
about all this: is she really ready, will she be accepted, will she do okay? Accepted she is, happy
she is, ready she thinks she is, and then suddenly
it is the night before school starts.

Her mother hears Ruth sobbing in her bedroom and rushes in to find out what is wrong.

"What if I can't find the class!"

"Your brother will show you where it is."

"What if he doesn't know where it is!" Ruth is a worrier. Lying in bed, she is making up stories to torture herself.

Her mother agrees to go with her to school the next morning. Mother goes back to bed briefly and then hears Ruth sobbing again.

"What if I can't find my desk!"

Ruthie spends much of the rest of the night imagining disaster and sobbing as if the disaster is already occurring.

The next morning Ruth, her mother, and her brother find Ruth's room and her seat. She comes home exultant. She loved everything she did that day and falls asleep quite happily in the middle of dinner.

Her basic worry seemed to be, "What if I prove to be too young for the first grade?" Because she attached this worry to the tangibles of the room and desk, she stopped worrying as soon as they were found. Jean forgot about boils as soon as the siege ended, but spent several years worrying about her nighttime ITs.

Bill's school worries were more like the boil-lancing trauma, in that they were based on reality. His school troubles lasted longer than the boils and were the basis for lifetime worries that he'd be a failure.

Bill is a sweet little guy, who had no trouble learning to add but he can't seem to get the hang of multiplication. He and his father struggle together over what his father believes is a simple task: the memorization of the multiplication tables from the ones through the twelves. Bill is stuck on the sixes.

He's been stuck there for what seems to him and his father to be a very long time.

The teacher has a game she calls Multiplication Baseball. The kids line up in two teams, and she pitches the ball: "What's four times eight?" The batter answers, and if he's right, he's on first base. Three outs, and the other team is up. Whenever Bill is at bat, he and all the other kids know, even before the teacher throws him the problem, that he'll make an out for his team. Now it's his turn again, and all the kids groan.

"What's six times six?"

"Forty?" he hopes out loud. And he's out and slinks back to his seat.

It's just as bad on the days when the teacher calls on people to write down answers to the problems she's written on the board. Just about everybody else will get the problems right. He doesn't raise his hand, he looks away, he prays that she won't see him, and on some blessed days he gets all the way through math, safely into geography, without going to the board. In geography he does okay. But the worst, the very worst is happening today. Everybody else is waving arms and hands like windmills, and Judy is yelling, "I know! I know!" And the teacher calls on Bill.

Bill walks to the blackboard, doomed. It doesn't do any good to write down a number. Everybody will laugh. There are so many numbers in the world, you just can't ever guess right. He reads the problem, in his teacher's clear, perfect writing: 5×5. In despair, he remembers that he knows that one. He knows his fives. But not today. Five times five, he mutters softly, and there is not one single answer in his head.

At home he worries about Multiplication Baseball and math on the board, and the more he thinks about it, the worse he feels. Supper, TV, nothing is fun anymore as he is caught in his hopeless worries about the next day at school.

Many worries are based on real events, like painful boils and the mortification of multiplication. Others are fears of the unknown, like the first day of the first grade. The early imaginary worries, like Jean's ITs, are of unknown origin, and theorists have a great time making up explanations that will bolster their own particular theories of human behavior. Perhaps the IT worriers have less overt trauma or perhaps they simply have a flair for the dramatic.

Jean no longer believes in ITs, although a creak in the wall can be a murderer. However, she's reading a third-grade book about a forest fire and now she lies tight and worried in her bed, imagining forest fires and planning how to save herself when all around her the trees are burning.

She imagines running as fast as she can, jumping over logs and scrambling downhill. Down or up? Down, because you can run faster. WHAT IF the fire is down and she is up? She runs as fast as she can uphill, and the fire is hot and crackling and ahead of her is a stream. That'll save her! She jumps in the stream and finds a deep spot where the water will cover her, and at the very instant the fire sweeps past, she ducks under and holds her breath. She does this under the covers several times, practicing. Winning against the fire is exciting, but WHAT IF? WHAT IF she can't hold her breath long enough? Is it better to die from drowning or burning? She decides to plaster mud from the bottom of the creek all over her face and breathe through a hollow weed stem.

In her room there is no light, no sound anywhere, and she can't get the crackle of imaginary fire out of her ears. She certainly is too big to call her mother. She lies hot and rigid in the hot summer night. The WHAT IFs have replaced the ITs.

Jean is a worrier and she knows that her worries are ridiculous, which is why she keeps them secret from everyone. Her parents would laugh if they knew she worried about forest fires, when the nearest forest is five hundred miles away. She suffers anyway. Later, when she is twelve and taking Junior Lifesaving at the local swimming pool, she lies in her bed at night, thinking about artificial respiration.

She is alone, walking beside a lake, and there in the water is a handsome, drowning man, unconscious, obviously in need of artificial respiration. All by herself, she manages to drag him out of the water and onto the sand. She clears out his mouth, makes sure he hasn't swallowed his tongue, rolls him onto his stomach, places her hands on his back, begins to lean forward, her weight on his back, doing it exactly the way she's been taught, and just as the story begins to be wonderful, that old WHAT IF appears. WHAT IF he needs artificial respiration but he also has a broken back? Jean leans forward again, just right, hands on his back, and swings her weight forward onto him, pushing out his breath to ready him for his life-giving inspiration of air. Instantly her movements kill him, because of his broken back.

She finds no escape from the worry of that scene, and the next day during Junior Lifesaving class she asks the teacher what to do if a person needs artificial respiration and has a broken neck or broken back. (This is years before the Red Cross begins to teach mouth-to-mouth artificial respira-

tion.) The eighteen-year-old teacher, who just graduated from high school and will go to college after
the summer is over, and with whom Jean is very
secretly in love, says, "Never happens." She persists,
and the teacher says, "You think of the dumbest
things." Jean is totally humiliated. However, in order to vanquish that WHAT IF, she still needs to
know: if somebody has a broken neck or a broken
back and requires artificial respiration, whatever
should one do?

CHAPTER 3

COPYING THE FAMILY WORRIERS

Sometimes it seems as if the Ruths and Bills and Jeans of the world pick up the ability to worry without any outside help, just from the events in their lives, such as boils and multiplication tables. From time to time, all children anticipate the future with dread. No one can go through childhood without some anticipated unhappiness, even if it's only a trip to the dentist or the knowledge that father is going to find out that you've broken the head off his hammer. Some children grow up with real trauma. Will my father or mother come home drunk and abusive? Who will take care of me, now that my father has left and my mother is dying? Yesterday's bombs killed everybody next door and tomorrow's bombs may kill us. Children who grow up in truly terrible situations may need considerable help resolving and putting to rest their early traumas, but, surprisingly, these children are not necessarily the worriers of the world.

Most children do not learn to worry because of childhood trauma. They learn to worry because they grow up listening to and copying the worriers around them.

Jean's mother, Gloria, had a wondrous assortment of worries. In fact, she could find a worry for any

event in their lives. Jean can scarcely remember a
home subject that was not used for worry. If someone was late for dinner, there might have been an
accident. When company was coming, the worries
ranged from what the noninvited would feel to the
possible disaster of burned casseroles or children's
messy bedrooms.

One of her worries was secret and special, and
shared only with Jean. It was a WHAT IF. "What if
there is no money for college when you are old
enough to go?" Jean first heard this worry when
she was starting grade school, and through the years
it became so familiar that she could repeat it word
for word with all its variations.

The story begins with a recital of the joys of
college. Growing up in America, Gloria was a young
girl with a German last name during a bad time for
such names, World War I. But when she arrived at
college, the war was over, her name was forgiven,
she pledged a sorority, met Jean's father, Les, and
for four years lived like a princess in a sorority
house that looked like a castle. At college she
danced, partied, went canoeing, and studied English literature. Jean had seen the sorority and the
lake beside it, and she knew from Gloria that no
matter what else went on in life, having been to
college made it all worthwhile.

After describing college, Gloria would sigh, hug
Jean close to her, and talk of the Depression. "What
will we do if the Depression keeps on and on?"
Gloria would remind Jean that the family's weekly
newspaper might fail, just the way the banks failed.
"If the newspaper fails, how can you and your sisters go to college?"

In reality, this was a strange worry. Jean's college days were years away. Besides, Gloria and Les
were not in desperate circumstances. They bar-

tered free groceries for free ads and also bartered free laundry service, free clothes, free movies, and even free summer camp for Jean and her younger sister. Gloria's Uncle Adolf sent money, her Auntie Ida and her mother made whatever clothes couldn't be obtained through barter, and on both sides of the family there was enough money, in a pinch, to keep any little weekly newspaper afloat even in these worst of times. However, Jean didn't think the worry strange, since children tend not to look critically at parental worries.

The facts certainly didn't stop Gloria from worrying. She talked of all the ways they could be reduced to poverty and all the reasons why Jean must go to college. They would both think of things they could sell and jobs they could look for futilely. Finally the end of the story would come, and it was always the same dramatically tragic but college-saving solution. Gloria would say, "If I have to, I'll take in laundry and scrub floors!" Both Jean and Gloria knew that this was the ultimate sacrifice, since they both detested housework. During the years in which they worried together, Gloria never had to do either job, as the maid did the floors and barter got the laundry done.

Although at first Jean appreciated the love that went into this imagined sacrifice, eventually she became bored and angry. She was a worry addict like her mother, but in her worries of the fires and the broken backs and necks, she certainly never ended them by volunteering to scrub floors.

Years later she learned one reason why Gloria was a worrier. It all involved a blueberry patch and Great-Uncle Adolf's second wife, to whom he was married briefly before Jean was born.

One summer afternoon when Gloria's and Adolf's families were vacationing together, Gloria's mother found Gloria's father kissing Uncle Adolf's wife, right there in the blueberries. This one scene, in a lifetime of fidelity, was enough to make Gloria's mother worry about abandonment. She'd ask Gloria, "Who would you pick to live with, your father or me, if your father left us?" Gloria and her mother worried throughout Gloria's childhood. Gloria told this story to Jean on the eve of Gloria's parents' sixtieth wedding anniversary.

Jean wondered what worry stories her grandmother had been told when she was a child that taught her to be a worrier.

There are lots of ways parents tell their children to worry. See if any of the following invitations to become a worrier are familiar to you:

"What if..."

"You never know when lightning will strike!"

"Someday you won't be so lucky!"

"Watch out!"

"Be careful!"

"Troubles come in threes!"

"When you're a mother, you'll know what it is to worry!"

"If you feel too good, something bad is sure to happen!"

"A person can't help worrying about..."

"The time to worry is when everything seems to be going right."

"I worry myself sick about you kids!"

"This job is one big worry!"

"Troubles come when you're not looking!"

"It's crazy not to worry about . . ."

"You kids be quiet. Your father is worried about something."

"If you don't worry, you must not care."

"It's the things you don't worry about that happen."

"Just when you think everything is going well, all hell breaks loose."

"If you expect the worst, you'll never be disappointed."

From sayings such as these, families weave their worry myths. Do any of the following fit your family's beliefs?

- Worrying keeps your worries from coming true.
- Other people make you worry.
- Events make you worry.
- If you care, you worry.
- If you love, you worry.
- If you are sensitive, you worry.
- If you are intelligent, you worry.
- If you are human, you worry.

In spite of all these invitations to worry, you don't have to give in. But before you stop worrying, use the worry test and the chapters that follow in part II, to learn why you chose your particular worries. From your worries you can identify any "stuck spots" in your development. You'll learn ways to get unstuck and to make significant changes in yourself.

Then, in part III, you'll learn how to let your worries go.

PART II

CHAPTER 4

THE WORRY TEST: 100 WORRY QUESTIONS AND WHAT THEY MEAN FOR YOU

The test you are about to take will show you your worry clusters, which are groups of worries around a central theme. When you discover your worry clusters, you can use them to understand yourself better and to change your life.

Have you ever wondered why you choose to worry about certain things and not others? Of course, you worry when some traumatic event is about to take place, such as surgery or loss of your job. These are worries in response to problems in your life. In addition, you worry in response to things you decided about yourself and others long ago.

You were told who and what you were: "Mommy's helper," "Daddy's littlest baby," "the smartest kid you'll ever meet," "the accident we never planned for," "a real good kid who takes care of himself," "a joy," "a pain," "a little doll," "a tough guy." Early in your life you began to assimilate what others said about you.

You made positive and negative decisions about yourself based on these early statements about you, plus all the multitudinous events in your life, and on your own genetic predispositions.

Lots of these decisions were positive, such as "I'm special," "I'm lovable," "I'm the best reader in class," "I'm a good worker." You also made positive decisions about others. "Teachers are nice and they help me be smart," "My dad is my pal," "I help my brother and he helps me." Other decisions were not positive: "I'm never going to get what I want," "I'm only important when I take care of the others," "There's something wrong with me," "I'll never cry, because I'm a boy!" You may have made negative decisions about others, such as "You can't trust fathers because they leave you," "Other people are no good because they have a different color skin," "Other people are smarter than I am," "If I don't want to get hurt, I'd better play by myself, because other people are dangerous."

Within the areas of your positive decisions, you won't find worry clusters, except when something goes wrong. The girl who grows up knowing, "My dad and I are pals," will worry when her father is awaiting results of a biopsy, but won't cluster her worries around her father's health when he is obviously well, unless she also made negative decisions such as "I'll always need my daddy, because I can't make it on my own," or "I've got to be perfect, or daddy may die."

These early child decisions can rule a person's life, even when the person has no memory at all of making them. Just as you learned the rules of driving and continue to follow them automatically, so, too, you may drive through life automatically using the rules you accepted in childhood. It's as if you put on a psychological straitjacket in childhood and then forgot to take it off. One of the best ways of finding out about your own early decisions is to explore your present worries.

Freud called dreams the royal road to the unconscious.

Worries are a royal road to the unconscious and to the conscious. Like dreams, you write them unconsciously. Unlike dreams, you write them when you are awake, so your conscious mind is also involved. Even when the unconscious parts come "in code," you can learn to unravel the code easily. Your worries can tell you more fully than dreams what is going on in your psyche. Once you are aware of what is going on, you can take off whatever straitjacket you've been wearing. The following chapters will show you how.

But first, the test.

THE WORRY TEST

This is a list of one hundred common worries, with numbers after each worry. When you find a worry that is similar to your worries, write the worry number and the numbers that follow the worry. Example: "1. I worry about asking for a raise." If you worry about asking for a raise, a promotion, or a different job assignment, write "1" and after it, "12, 16, 18." When you have finished, read the explanation that follows the test.

1. I worry about asking for a raise. 12, 16, 18.
2. When everything's going great, I start to worry. 9, 11.
3. I worry that something's wrong with me. 8, 13, 15.
4. I have a serious illness and I worry about it. 20, 21.
5. I worry about getting wrinkles. 5, 9.
6. I worry about heaven. How will I choose between my two spouses, who'll both be there? 9.
7. I worry (unrealistically) about AIDS. 6, 9.
8. I have AIDS and I worry about my future. 21.

9. I worry that nobody will ever love me. 17.
10. I worry about money. (I have lots.) 9, 11, 18.
11. I worry about the stock market. 9, 10, 11.
12. I worry about money. (I don't have enough to meet my basic needs.) 10, 19.
13. I worry about my grown children. 9, 14.
14. I worry what my little children will be like when they are grown. 9, 11, 14.
15. I worry that my lover will leave me. 12, 15, 16, 17.
16. I worry about not fitting in at work. 10, 12, 13, 18.
17. I worry that people will see me blushing. 8, 12, 13, 15.
18. I worry that I'll be raped again. 20.
19. I worry about giving a speech in public. 10, 12, 15.
20. I worry that people don't accept me. 13, 15.
21. I worry that somebody will cheat me. 17, 18.
22. I worry that people like me only for my money. 13, 17, 18.
23. My worries make me wish I were dead. 19.
24. I worry because I don't know what to do. 7, 10, 19, 21.
25. I worry because I have more to do than I can possibly manage. 10, 14.
26. I worry about how I look when my lover and I dance. 9, 14.
27. I worry about illnesses I don't have. 9, 15.
28. I worry about the illness I do have. 21.
29. I worry that I'm not worrying enough. 5, 6, 9.
30. I don't know, I worry a lot and my worries are vague. 5, 6, 7.
31. I worry because my spouse doesn't dress up. 14.
32. I worry that people won't do what they say they'll do. 9, 14, 16.
33. I worry that someone will come to visit when the house isn't clean enough. 7, 14.

34. I worry about what will happen to me when I'm old and helpless. 9, 14, 20, 21.

35. I worry that I'll end up a bag lady because I don't know how to support myself. 5, 6, 7, 11.

36. I worry about how I'll do in our next game. 11.

37. I worry about my looks. 5, 13, 17.

38. I worry that I'm not a good enough lover. 15, 17.

39. I worry about dying before my children are grown. 9, 14, 21.

40. I worry about my healthy children dying before I do. 9.

41. I worry that my new furniture won't look right in my apartment. 11.

42. Everything is fine today, but what about tomorrow? 9.

43. I worry that my friends don't really like me. 13, 15, 18.

44. I worry about foreign affairs, even though I don't know what's going on in the world. 6.

45. I worry about another earthquake (tornado, flood, etc.). 5, 20.

46. I worry about getting sued for something. 9, 17.

47. I worry that I am not like other people. 12, 13, 15.

48. I worry because I don't know what I want. 14, 16.

49. I worry because I don't have enough friends. 13, 17.

50. I worry because I can't find a man (or woman) to love. 17.

51. I worry about my grades (which are fine). 11.

52. I worry about my grades (which are not good). 5, 6, 10.

53. I worry that whatever I do, it'll be wrong. 6, 7, 15.

54. I worry about my smoking. 19.

55. I worry about my relatives' smoking. 14, 16.
56. I worry about the Bomb. 9, 18, 21.
57. I worry that I did my taxes wrong. 6.
58. I worry that others do better than I do. 5, 6, 10, 11.
59. I worry that I bought the wrong color coat. 7, 11, 16.
60. I worry about the bake sale I am managing. 11, 12.
61. I think about my worries, but I don't feel bad about them. 8.
62. When I worry, I get so sad I cry all afternoon. 19.
63. I worry whenever I have to make a choice about something. 7, 16.
64. I worry about my family (realistically). 14, 20, 21.
65. I worry that I am not as happy as I should be. 9, 14, 17.
66. I worry that I'll disappoint my family. 5, 15.
67. I worry that people don't approve of me. 13, 15.
68. My worries are all logical ones. 8.
69. I worry that my car (plumbing, roof repair) won't be done right. 12, 18.
70. I worry that if I get my way, they won't like me. 12, 16.
71. I worry that if I don't exercise more, someday I'll end up with a heart attack. 9, 11, 14, 15.
72. I worry that if I don't stop being late, people won't like me. 5, 7, 17.
73. I worry about finding a career before it's too late. 5, 6, 7, 10.
74. I worry that if I don't start dating, I'll never get married. 15, 17.
75. I worry that my favorite charity isn't getting enough money. 8, 15.
76. I worry that if I don't start flossing my teeth, I could end up with dentures. 5, 9.

77. I worry that I don't do enough for my grand-
    children. 14.
78. I worry about my drinking. 19.
79. I worry about a family member's drinking. 14,
    20, 21.
80. When I worry, I feel like killing myself. 19.
81. I worry that whatever I am doing isn't good
    enough. 11, 19.
82. Others do my worrying for me. 5.
83. I worry because I am ten pounds overweight.
    5, 6, 9.
84. I worry that my family will forget my birthday.
    16.
85. I worry about life in general. 9, 19.
86. I worry about the world and never about me.
    8, 14, 16.
87. I can use any old worry to depress myself. 19.
88. I worry about my high blood pressure (or
    other medical problem) but I don't do any-
    thing about it. 19.
89. I worry that someone will break into my house.
    6, 7, 9.
90. I worry that someone will break into my house
    again. 20.
91. I've never worried in my life. 8.
92. I worry that some of the bad things that have
    happened will happen again. 20.
93. I worry about things that I know are going to
    come true. 21.
94. I worry that when I get old, I'll be alone. 9, 17.
95. I worry about house fires, burglaries, rapes,
    assaults, and things like that. 5, 9, 17, 18, 20.
96. I worry about my presidential candidate. 14,
    16.
97. I worry about what's going on in other parts
    of the world. 9, 14, 21.
98. I worry that someday I'll show I'm angry. 8.
99. I worry that if I ask for what I want, I'll start
    to cry. 8, 16.

100. I worry that my nose (penis, thighs, hair, etc.)
      isn't like other people's. 13, 15.

With any of these worries, if you think about them
but don't have a feeling response, add number 8 to the
numbers you have written down. If you feel depressed
as you worry, add number 19. If you worry because you've
had a similar worry come true, add number 20.

If you know that your particular worry will definitely
occur, add number 21.

When you have finished, add up how many times you
have written the same number. If you have written a
number only once, you may ignore it. If you have written
a number two or three times, that may be a worry cluster.
If you have written a number more than three times, you
can be certain that this is a worry cluster that is important
for you to understand.

The numbers you have written refer to chapters in
this book that deal with particular worry clusters. If you
like, start with the chapters that apply to you. Each chapter
begins with several typical worries and how they relate
to early decisions you may have made about yourself and
others. Each chapter concludes with effective methods
for breaking free of those decisions. The methods for
breaking free may seem too simple, but try them anyway.
They can be very helpful to you. In fact, you may discover
that the suggestions in the following chapters help you
to make real changes in your life.

After you have read the chapters that apply to you,
you might enjoy reading the rest of the chapters in this
section, to learn about the early decisions others have
made.

Then, in part III, you'll learn how to use your worries
well in your life today and then to let them go.

CHAPTER 5

GROWING

"Sometimes I think about going back to college, because it was fun. Then I worry about, well, what if I don't want to finish? If I quit again, my big brother will really be mad, because he's the one who pays my tuition."

"My biggest worry is my wrinkles. I worry about being old and I can't stand the idea!"

"Now that Tom's dead, I just worry all the time. I don't know about insurance or cars or anything. I worry that everything will fall apart. There's no one to take care of things."

"I never need to worry because my lover does all the worrying for both of us."

"My best friend moved away, and now I worry all the time. She used to keep me doing the right things. Without her, I just don't know what to do."

I NEVER GREW UP

People who accept the message "Don't grow" may be the youngest in their families or the only child of doting parents. They are usually attractive, happy, and a pleasant distraction from the worries and troubles the rest of the family face. These "young ones" are given love for being cute rather than competent. No one says to them, "Wow, look how beautifully you take care of yourself!" or "That was a difficult job and you did it well." They are stifled with, "I'll do it for you" instead of "You can do it for yourself." When parents talk to them about the future, they say, "You can be anything you want," instead of, "You have to work hard to get the good jobs."

When they tell their worries, they expect someone else to come up with solutions. "I don't have the right dress for the party," one will say. Immediately Dad responds, "Don't worry, darling, your daddy will buy you one." Parents and friends say, "She doesn't have a care in the world!" These people, who don't grow up, are the Peter Pans and the Little Princesses.

They may go through life without significant worries as long as they have daddies, mommies, Wendys, or big brothers to take care of them. Their worries begin when their caretakers die or lose interest. Doting parents may decide to move to a first-class retirement village and stop supporting their thirty-year-old son. They send him the unpleasant news that if he continues toward his second Ph.D, he'll have to pay for it himself. Wendys join women's consciousness-raising groups and divorce Peter Pans. Big brothers transfer their interest to their own children. Sugar daddies desert Little Princesses to marry someone more interesting or someone younger and therefore more perfectly princessy.

When life does become difficult, they either find new caretakers or inundate themselves with worry. *Their worries are not helpful to them because they use them as an alternative to action.* A bewildered young man, who just flunked out of college, says, "Well, I did worry a lot about the exams." This means that if there were any justice under heaven, good grades would be given on a sliding scale for worry as well as for quality of exam papers.

Another young man who failed, said, "I guess I should have worried," as if that would have taken care of everything.

A childlike mother worries about not having presents for her children for Christmas, but doesn't make gifts for them or attend garage sales in order to pick up presents she can afford. She thinks she has done all that could be expected of her, simply because she has worried. Some people will agree with her and say, "The poor dear is so worried about Christmas!" Someone may even pity her enough to buy the presents for the children.

The worries of childlike people are repetitions of the theme "I'm helpless" and reinforce their beliefs that they can do nothing to protect themselves.

As they grow older, they worry excessively about wrinkles, gray hair, and any other sign that their bodies are aging. For a while, they may get by with plastic surgery, hair dye, diets, and exercise, but they continue to worry about signs of age. Some people's refusal to mature is entirely focused on their bodies. They do succeed in their careers, do not need help from others, and the only sign that they are stuck in this syndrome is their refusal to like themselves as they age.

"I'M GROWN AND GROWING"

If you are one of the Peter Pans or Little Princesses, recognize that you have already started to grow and change just by the fact that you have read this far.

Let yourself remember your assets. You learned to play and to have fun, knew joy as a child, and you didn't burn yourself out working from the time you could walk. You know how to be delightful, young, and entertaining, and all of those qualities are admirable. You liked blowing bubbles and playing TV games instead of mowing every lawn in the neighborhood for less than minimum wage. You are an interesting friend and you are capable of teaching the male and female Wendys how to fly. If you've let your present situation or your worried predictions of the future take away from your zest, it's time to give yourself loving permission to rediscover the joyful you.

Remind yourself that you were loved. It may not have felt like love all the time, because the love you received may have been buried under tons of advice, but nevertheless the fact remains that you were loved. Only the loved are given parental permission and encouragement to stay young.

Will you love yourself as you take charge of your own growth? Let yourself remember what you were like at a time when you were learning something new. Remember the thrill of learning to swim, to read, to hit the ball with the bat. Remember the first time you built a birdhouse or rode a bicycle or programmed a computer. If you don't remember, let yourself imagine a happy scene in which you are proud of your accomplishment. Pretend you are that child and practice saying, "I did it!" Feel the excitement of success and then congratulate yourself for what you did.

You might like to "bring yourself up" all over again in fantasy. Start at the age you learned to walk and pretend you remember. Watch yourself as a baby, wobbling across the room and clapping your hands with delight at being able to walk. Pretend the baby falls down and then stands up without any help from anybody. Congratulate the baby and let yourself be joyous that this baby will keep on growing, learning, and doing.

Every night, before you go to sleep, pretend the baby is a year older and relive or imagine accomplishments for that age. Really applaud yourself for accomplishments and independence.

As you "regrow" yourself, you may suddenly remem-

ber a scene in which your growth was stymied. June
remembers a scene when she was twelve.

She is sitting in her bedroom, hemming her skirt.
This is a brand-new activity for her and she's concentrating hard on doing it right. She's never cared
about skirt lengths before, because her mommy and
her big sister always chose her clothes for her.
Today she wants a very short skirt, like the high
school girls wear, and that is why she is shortening
one of her old skirts. She believes she's big enough
to look like a teenager and she wants very much
to be stylish. She's sewing as fast as she can, trying
to get it done before anyone finds out.

In the midst of her hemming, her big sister
comes into her room. June remembers the scene
as if it were yesterday. Her sister says, "What are
you doing? Look at how you're wrecking your
skirt." She shows June that the thread is pulled too
tight. June looks at the crinkles in the hem and feels
a kind of despair. She starts to cry. Her sister pulls
out the thread, saying, "I'll fix it for you. You
wouldn't look good in a short skirt anyway. You're
too little." June gives up and continues to be a
sweetly compliant younger daughter.

When June recognizes that scene as the story of her
life, she decides to change. In her imagination, she tells
the twelve-year-old, "Your sister is wrong. You are not
too young. Get the thread and hem that skirt!" June imagines a new ending for the scene and then looks for
changes she wants to make in her present life.

If you find such scenes, tell yourself that you don't
need to be stuck. Write a new ending and see how you
can make it apply to your life today. In fantasy you might
talk to your parents or your brothers and sisters about

your new decision to grow. "I am not staying stuck at age eight. Even if you loved me best at that age, I am moving on." "I tried to stay an adolescent, because that was a wonderful time for me. But no more. I've outgrown those years."

Perhaps others still want you to be helpless. That is their problem. Don't sabotage yourself by believing that you can't change until others treat you differently. You can change no matter what anyone else in your universe does.

Today, when you've finished reading this chapter, let yourself look for solutions rather than for worries. Brag to yourself about anything new you have learned or done today. If you like, you can find whole new areas in which to grow. One woman bought herself a computer for her seventieth birthday and hired a college student to teach her to use it. Another woman is taking auto mechanics. A man bought himself a sewing machine and makes "animals that never were but ought to be" to give to child care centers. Lots of people work hard at causes that are important to them. What growth would you applaud in you?

Some people who have remained immature have accumulated severe reality problems, because they haven't learned to balance a checkbook, to support themselves, or to be the kind of parent their children need. If this is true of you, take care of your important problems first, as best you can. You may need real help, rather than the mixed-up help you have been getting. An important aspect of growing is finding and accepting the professional help you may need from doctors, lawyers, bankers, psychotherapists, or others. Evaluate the professional helpers carefully, however, and *run, do not walk, to the nearest exit* if your helpers are patronizing or try to do your thinking for you.

If you are a worrier about your physical appearance because you want to look forever sixteen, you owe yourself the joy of appreciating yourself at your present age. How will you do that? How will you let yourself know that all ages have their own particular beauty? One of the nicest aspects of real maturity is that you can appreciate yourself at your current age. You can look in the mirror and see a friend. Try it. Go to your mirror and smile. Say, "Hi, friend," to yourself.

CHAPTER 6

THINKING

"Oh, I don't know, I guess I mostly worry because I'm not getting anywhere. I should plan. I've got to figure out how to get a better job, but I can't seem to think what to do."

"I worry about the IRS, you know. I don't know why I worry about taxes, because, you know, I don't make much money and, anyway, I just take all my paystubs to the IRS and they figure it out for me. But, you know, I can't understand any of the things they tell me, and I worry about that."

"I worry that I'm not very smart. I don't know, I just don't have anything to say at parties."

"Of course, I worry about foreign affairs. But I don't really know what's going on."

"I CAN'T THINK"

People who believe that they can't think announce this belief to the world by way of their statements: "I can't think," "I don't know," and "You know." Often they smile when they affirm their inability to think or know. If it were true that they can't think or know, this would be nothing to smile about!

They say, "You know," just as they did when they were children and others did know more. They nod so that you will nod back. Very early they were taught to doubt their own knowledge and their thinking ability until mother or teacher affirmed their thoughts by nodding to the statement "you know." The "you know" then becomes automatic, like a stutter: "You know, I have this cousin on the East Coast, you know, who, I don't know, seems, you know, to be having trouble with her marriage, you know." The listeners, who have never heard of this cousin before, find themselves nodding and smiling affirmation that the speaker does not know this cousin but they, the listeners do. In just this way, parents and teachers nodded affirmation in the past.

Children are taught to doubt their ability to think. Mothers and fathers who do their children's homework are saying both: "You can't think" and "You don't have to think because I'll do your thinking for you." Parents also give their children messages by example. A mother says to her daughter, "Ask your father about math. It's beyond me." Or she says, "I got along fine my entire life without algebra or geometry." This tells her daughter that if she wants to be like mother, she will not think about math.

Parents who doubt their own intelligence sometimes threaten a child who is thinking clearly. "Don't be a smart-ass!" or "Don't get too big for your britches!" Parents may need to win arguments so badly that they belittle any new facts or new thinking a child displays. Older brothers and sisters project their own self-doubts onto the younger ones, saying, "You don't know anything!"

Children may learn to confuse worrying with thinking when they hear a parent say, "If I didn't worry about the cost of living, you wouldn't have food on your plate!"

In some families attributes are distributed like playing cards, one to a person, and no one gets an attribute already assigned to another child. If sister is considered bright, she has cornered the market on brains. Another child may be sweet, good-looking, nice, musical, or athletic, but not bright.

Our culture abounds in antithinking messages:

"Don't worry your pretty little head about that."

"Boys don't like girls who are too smart."

"Let daddy show you how to do your homework."

"Nobody in our family can spell."

"Do it because I told you to!"

"Geniuses aren't popular."

"Don't be so smart!"

"Don't ask so many questions."

"Mother is not drunk, she's just tired, so don't think about it."

"Don't criticize your mother (father, teachers, minister, government, president, God)."

"Don't read that book."

"Don't see that movie."

"Don't listen to that man, he sounds like a Commie."

"Don't think about poverty, inequality, family secrets, or sex."

"Don't think, buy" (say the advertising slogans).

"Buy now, think later" (say the credit cards).

"DON'T THINK ABOUT IT!"

In addition, we have all trained ourselves to survive and stay happy by giving ourselves antithinking messages whenever thinking becomes too painful. When Jean's grandson, Brian, was three years old, she used to chat with him by telephone. One day he began the conversation with, "Hello, Gramma, did you know people eat pigs!" He had just learned that his pig friend down the street had been murdered in order to be made into bacon and hot dogs, which he'd always loved. He agonized about his pig friend for a few days, refused all meat, and then did what people do. He stopped thinking about pigs.

"Don't think about it!" is the tragic message given children in dysfunctional families. Children are not supposed to think about the fact that a parent is alcoholic, mentally ill, or sexually abusive. Children learn to curtail their thinking in order to avoid any unpleasant truth about their families.

If you substitute worry for thinking, or confuse yourself rather than using your brain to solve problems, perhaps you were told from the beginning that you couldn't think as well as other people. Some children don't receive the special tutoring they need. If they have a learning disability that makes it difficult to learn to read or to conceptualize, they may believe they are stupid, because there is no one in their school who knows how to teach them. The fact is, they are no more stupid than nearsighted children, who can't read what is written on the blackboard until they are given glasses. Some children think they are stupid because they are expected to read English before they even speak the language, and some just didn't seem to have a chance to think and learn.

While Abraham was in the federal penitentiary in Marion, Illinois, he graduated from high school and college by taking correspondence courses and was about to receive his master's degree in counseling psychology. Under a specially funded program, he was permitted to study

and then to counsel other inmates. This is how he tells
the story of his education:

> "I always had this under-70 IQ. When I was a kid,
> they put me in special classes, where you color and
> paste and never learn anything. They said I couldn't
> think. Well, the truth is, a lot of things were going
> on in my life that you wouldn't call pleasant. I don't
> suppose I had time for thinking, because I was too
> busy trying not to be killed. I'm talking about from
> as far back as I can remember. When I got old
> enough, I joined the army. I was still under-70 and
> I couldn't really read and write, so I wasn't eligible
> for any training the army had. I did some terrible
> things and I got sent here, and I met the prison
> psychiatrist. He was the first person in my life who
> didn't believe I was too dumb to learn. He said,
> 'Man, you spent your life acting dumb, but you are
> not dumb.' So he got me studying, and they let me
> study day and night. I was an under-70 fool when
> I came in, and after I started studying, they tested
> me again and I was 90. I kept on studying, and my
> IQ kept growing, and right now my IQ is 129 and
> going up all the time!"

"I'M THINKING!"

If you want to affirm your own thinking, the first step is
very simple. Listen to yourself. Decide you will eliminate
antithinking statements from your vocabulary: "I can't
think," "I don't know," "I'm confused," and "You know."
If you find listening to yourself difficult, use a tape recorder to listen to your speech. Then set to work to
change it. Put "I know," "I think," and "I believe" into
your conversations.

Next, you can use worries to prove to yourself that you can and do think. Begin with someone else's worry. If you are a good auto mechanic, pick the worry "I keep worrying that there is something wrong with my car." Imagine a man or woman saying this to you, and then imagine yourself explaining how to think creatively about cars.

If you handle your checkbook well, tell an imaginary someone how to think about money and budgets. Now congratulate yourself for thinking well. It is not that you "can't think," but that you have chosen to solve some problems and not others. A therapy group practiced this method of problem solving.

Jane says, "I worry because I need to figure out how to get a better job." Sue says, "I worry about my health." Dan says, "I worry about the IRS." And Richard says, "My biggest worry is bills." They are stuck in the rut of their own worries and have not found solutions. In the group each member is asked to write his or her worry on a piece of paper and pass it to the person on the right. That person has one minute to think about the problem and write down suggestions for solving it before passing it on. The next person also has a minute to jot down additional suggestions. When everyone has written on the sheets of paper, they are returned to the worriers.

The group discusses how easy it is to think up good suggestions for others. They decide this is because they don't substitute worry for thinking, and they don't belittle their own creativity by saying, "Yes, but" or "That will never work," when thinking about other people's problems.

Jane comments, "I don't think the solution is to expect to solve every problem," and immediately hears her "I don't think" message. She changes the wording to, "I do think that the solution is to solve the problems I can, and not to judge myself stupid because some problems are still unsolvable." She smiles. "Yes, I do think that. I think! That is the important message I am giving myself."

Richard recognizes that his suggestions to others are excellent and decides, "I give myself lousy suggestions because I don't want to sacrifice in order to pay my bills. This has nothing to do with inability to think. It has to do with refusing to think about a budget, because a budget will restrict my pleasures." He sighs and then decides to make a budget that suits him and find a way to enjoy the process.

Sue decides that she doesn't have to know all about medicine, when she is not a physician. She can find a physician she trusts.

They all recognize that in the past they substituted worrying for thinking in their own problem areas, and not in others. They decide to believe in their abilities to think and then to expand their expertise.

In a later group session Dan, who worries about the IRS, imagines that organization to be as difficult as his father was when he was young. Dan remembers his father yelling at him, "Think!" until the very word became its opposite. In an imaginary conversation with his father, he explains this and says, "I'm only a little boy and when you yell, 'Think,' I'm so scared of you that I can't think of anything except that you might hit me." As he talks, Dan experiences his early terror and also experiences his inability to think what to do next.

He says to his therapy group, "I honestly am confused. Just imagining his face gets me uptight. I don't know what to think. I'm going to stop now."

Sue reminds him that he is behaving in group exactly as he described behaving with his father. He is confusing himself and stopping himself from solving his problem.

A few sessions later Dan is ready to finish. Again he fantasizes seeing his father on the chair in front of him. He says, "You were a mean son of a bitch. I hated you!" He stands up and pounds a pillow with his fist as he declares very clearly, "I'm not afraid of you anymore. You aren't twice my size anymore. I am taller and stronger than you. You're a little old man today, and you're not real bright." Dan sits back and says, "That's true. You weren't real bright and you never did take any courses in child rearing. You probably just treated me the way you were treated." Dan forgives his father and reports feeling very calm. The next day, as an experiment, he goes to the local office of the Internal Revenue Service and questions them about some of the new income tax laws. He is amazed at his own ability to listen, to think, and to ask good questions.

The sequence for believing in your own ability to think is:

1. Change your vocabulary to tell the world that you think, believe, and know.
2. Recognize the areas in which you think well.
3. Congratulate yourself for your problem-solving abilities instead of putting yourself down whenever you can't solve a problem.
4. If you still feel stupid, go back to the past as Dan did and let the old scenes go.

5. Get expert help in areas that are beyond your own expertise.
6. Let yourself know that thinking is a joyous mental activity.

It's not necessarily fun to think about budgets and the IRS. In fact "thinking" can seem arduous if you connect it only with thinking about boring things. Encyclopedias are dull if you are using them to look up facts you've never wanted to know. They are exciting when you are excited about what you are learning from them. How long has it been since you've leafed through an encyclopedia just for fun?

CHAPTER 7

DOING

"I worry whenever I have to buy something. I saw this blouse I liked, but then I began to worry 'What if it's on sale next week?' If I buy it today and it goes on sale next week, I will have wasted money. So I walked out of the store, and then I began to worry that by next week it will be sold and I won't have it at all. I hate making decisions!"

"For ten years I've thought about leaving the priesthood. The problem is, whatever decision I make, I worry that it'll be a mistake. I worry that, if I leave, I'll be sorry."

"I think about getting a better job. But what if I leave this job and then get fired from the next one? What if there's a nationwide depression? I don't know what to do."

"My sister is a difficult woman. Three years ago I wrote her a letter telling her exactly what I think of her. Ever since I wrote it, I've worried about whether or not to send it."

"I'M AFRAID TO DECIDE"

The message, loud and clear, is "Don't do!" It's okay to think, to worry, to obsess, but not to take action:

"Think before you speak."

"Look before you leap."

"Don't rock the boat."

"If you make your bed, you'll have to lie in it."

"Are you sure?"

"Better safe than sorry."

"Marry in haste, repent at leisure."

"Be careful!"

"Don't make waves."

"Hang your clothes on a hickory limb, but don't go near the water!"

These are messages given by fearful and overprotective parents, in a misguided attempt to keep their children safe. They are afraid for their children to learn to skate, swim, date, or leave home. They teach that life is dangerous and that mistakes can never be undone. They say, "Perhaps you'd better think about it some more," instead of, "Go to it, honey!"

Do you substitute worry for action? Do you worry about the risks of doing? Of course there are risks involved in any change. There are also risks in nonchange. It is fine to assess both the risks and the advantages of taking action. The worrier, substituting worry for action, weighs the positives and the negatives, and then weighs and weighs and weighs and weighs.

Jeri comes for therapy because she is unhappy with her marriage and wants "the strength to get a divorce." She's been thinking of divorce for six years and has done nothing except worry about the future with her husband or without him. Her complaint is that her husband works long hours during the week and watches the TV sports channel weekends. She feels cheated. She has used every method she knows to make him change, including anger, depression, and attempts at bargaining.

In therapy she is asked to try an experiment. "Close your eyes and pretend it is a year from today. You left this office, moved out of the house, and filed for divorce immediately. Now it's been a year since you have lived with your ex-husband. Your divorce is final. Imagine where you are living, what you are doing, and how you are feeling." Jeri imagines that she is working in the city and is still miserable. "I feel sad and guilty for divorcing. I'm not doing anything, really. I'm worried about my future. I miss Larry."

Next she imagines what she is doing, thinking, and feeling a year from today if she is still with Larry. He continues to work long hours and spend his weekends watching TV. What is she thinking, feeling, and doing? "This is intolerable. I am enraged that I am still with him. I'm lonely. I'm worried about my future and all I'm doing is waiting for Larry to change."

As she thinks about her two fantasies, she realizes that she is programming herself to be sad, angry, and lonely and to substitute misery for action. No wonder she is stuck in her worries! Her goal in therapy becomes, "I'll learn to do rather than to be miserable. I'll find actions that I'll be happy with and I won't be lonely." She agrees to put off her divorce until she is successful in taking charge of her own happiness.

She begins to make changes in her own life. She calls friends and makes luncheon dates with them.

At first she keeps finding people like herself, people who blame others for their dissatisfactions in life. In therapy she recognizes that her dissatisfaction with these friends is a result of changes she is making in herself. She no longer likes spending time with friends who bad-mouth their husbands.

Jeri looks for new activities. While her husband watches TV, she hikes in the woods with her new camera and teaches herself microphotography of wildflowers. She enjoys this hobby so much that she enrolls in weekend photography courses, where she meets new friends who are active rather than obsessive. The fascinating turnaround occurs when her husband becomes unhappy that she is neglecting him. At this point he decides to join her in therapy, and they work together on making a satisfying marriage for themselves. If her husband had not changed, she might or might not have ended the marriage. Either way, her success came from doing rather than worrying unhappily. She took charge of her own life.

If you are fence-sitting instead of decision making, perhaps you, too, are programming yourself to be miserable no matter what choice you make. If you don't change jobs, you believe you are stuck forever with poor pay and no challenge. If you change, you worry that you are in the last-hired, first-fired group. If you don't marry, you worry that your lover will get tired of waiting and leave you. If you marry, you worry that your lover will turn into a nag like your mother or your father. If you buy the shoes, they will turn out to be too bright for the fall season. If you don't buy them, you'll never find another pair that matches your suit so well.

When you find yourself caught up in obsessive worrying, remind yourself that your worry is designed to keep you from achieving rather than to help you achieve. It is a straitjacket that prevents action. For you, thinking, planning, trying to choose, analyzing, talking, and writing, are all nonsolutions. The solution is action.

"FULL STEAM AHEAD"

Each time you begin to go over your same old worry, see if you are giving yourself any new information by worrying. If not, take a small, imperfect action. Apply for a job that isn't the perfect job for you. Buy the pair of shoes and decide that you will enjoy them for thirty days and then give them to Goodwill, so that someone else can also enjoy them. Find a new activity to do with your lover and let yourself believe that it doesn't matter if you both enjoy it a little or a lot.

Congratulate yourself for carrying out new actions and, again, don't expect perfection. You are learning a new way of life, to do rather than to obsess, and not all of your actions will necessarily please you. That's okay. When a person is learning to play a violin, each sound made by the bow on the strings is not necessarily lovely.

To change, you need humor, daring, and especially self-encouragement. Self-analysis is contraindicated, because it can so easily become another way of obsessing instead of doing. If you decide to get help from a therapist, be sure your therapist is not obsessive. Lots are, which is why they choose a profession that involves studying and analyzing rather than doing. A good therapist for you is someone who practices brief or time-limited therapy. Such a person will help you move ahead by doing rather than by worrying.

The antidote to the "Don't do" straitjacket is action. The reckless people of the world need the slogan, "Don't just do something. Stand there." If you've been obeying that slogan and "standing there" for a long, long time, your slogan needs to be, "Damn the imaginary torpedos, full steam ahead."

CHAPTER 8

FEELING

"I am not sure what you mean by feel. I worry about making a profit in my new business. I plan. Feel? Well, I feel that if I don't make a profit, I will lose everything. Is that a feeling?"

"I do worry, of course, about the possibility of nuclear war. I don't have a feeling exactly. What should I feel?"

"I guess they are going to make me retire pretty soon, now that I'm almost seventy. No, I'm not worrying exactly, except I don't know how the hell I'll fill my time. I'm thinking about it, but I don't feel much of anything."

"I worry about my mother, who has Alzheimer's disease. I don't feel anything. What good would it do her if I fell apart?"

"I DON'T FEEL A THING"

Some children, especially boys, are raised to be "the strong, silent type," which means: "pretend to be strong by being silent about feelings." They do push-ups, lift weights, overdevelop the muscles in their jaws by gritting their teeth, and end up not quite knowing their own humanness. When asked what they feel, they answer, "I feel that . . ." and finish their sentence with a thought or a worry rather than an emotion. Because they have so blocked their emotions, they don't experience, "I am sad" or "scared" or "ashamed." On the rare occasion when inner feelings burst through their defenses, they rush away quickly so that no one will notice.

Some girls are raised to be "sugar and spice and everything nice," which means: "be scared and even sad, but never be angry." If you are super-strong or sugar-and-spice, you have been cheated out of your own natural emotions. You don't know it's okay for you to weep, blush, yell, and sometimes have a squeaky-scared voice.

Your worry may be about something terrible that you know will happen to you. You may be worrying because a loved one has an incurable disease. If you are supposed to be strong, how can you confide your fear and your sadness in a way that will bring you comfort or relief?

Your worry may be silly, totally "off the wall," such as worrying that you'll die alone when you've got six healthy, loving kids and a healthy, loving spouse. Even if you judge it silly, you have a right to know your own emotional response to what you tell yourself inside your head.

Your worry may be a fiercely hidden secret. You may be worried because you are losing your hair or your savings or your job, but you don't tell a soul because you don't dare let others know your emotions. You don't dare let yourself say, "I'm scared," or "I'm sad." The more intense your feelings may be, the more you suppress them, because you are especially unwilling to be seen sobbing or raging. Your fear of expressing your own emotions leaves you uncomforted, unhelped, and lonely.

For you, learning to stop worrying is premature. It's important that you first learn to recognize and share your emotional responses to your own worries. In that way, you can conquer your real fear, the fear of feeling. Are you willing?

"MY FEELINGS MAKE ME HUMAN"

Each time you find yourself worrying, whether it is a silly, "off the wall" worry or a real concern, say to yourself, "When I worry about this, I am . . ." and finish the sentence with one emotional word: "I am sad," "I am angry," "I am frightened," "I am ashamed," "I am happy." If you tend to use judgmental words, such as *stupid*, *guilty*, *nutty*, or *childish*, start with whatever judgmental word you use and then add your emotional response.

"When I worry about this, I call myself stupid." That is a judgment rather than an emotion, so add, "When I call myself stupid, I am sad." "When I worry about not having a better job, I judge myself guilty, and I am ashamed and also sad."

Some people invent worries in order to repress or change their feelings. Al worried about the economy, which wasn't hurting him particularly, so that he wouldn't have to recognize his own sadness that his son refused to join the family business.

In a worry workshop Marion says, "When my husband is late coming home from work, I worry about accidents and I am frightened." In therapy she is asked if this is her only emotional response to his lateness. At first she believes it is. "I worry that he is in an accident and is lying on the road, bleeding. I terrify myself with my worry." When asked if she is ever angry at him for coming home late, she says, "How can you be angry at someone you believe may be dying?" Then she admits that sometimes, when he walks in healthy and uninjured, she feels "a little anger mixed in with my relief." As she thinks more about this, she becomes more angry. "I AM angry! He could phone when he plans to be late. Yes, I am angry!" She begins to enjoy the power she feels when she says, "I am angry!"

After she admits to herself that she is angry at him for being late, she finds another emotion she has completely suppressed: jealousy. "I am jealous of him! I really am jealous. I want to be the one who comes home late and gets served dinner no matter when I breeze in. I want to have interesting things to do outside my own home! I want to be late, too!" When Marion allows herself to know her emotions, including jealousy, she feels very free. She discovers a new goal, to set up her life in such a way that she, too, has interesting things to do.

After you have practiced knowing your own feelings, it is important to be aware of how you express them. Trembling goes with fear, but smiles and tears and angry tones do not. Tears and an unhappy expression go with sadness, but smiles and trembling and an angry voice do not. A firm, loud voice, a frown, and decisive gestures go with anger, but tears and trembling and smiles do not.

Test yourself in front of a mirror. If you see yourself smiling as you say, "I am angry," real anger was probably a no-no when you were little, so you tried to cover it up with a smile. Allow yourself to express anger now and watch again in the mirror as you say, "I am angry." Explain your anger. "I am angry that you don't let me know when you'll be late for dinner." If you find yourself wanting to cry, that, too, is a way of avoiding your anger. Stay with anger, as if you are an actor training for the part of an angry person, until you can say, "I am angry," and show that anger by your facial expression, your voice tone, and your gestures.

If you grin as you say, "I am sad," remember that you are now a grown-up. People won't tease you, punish you, or fall apart today when you say what you feel. Or, if they do, that truly is their problem. Practice expressing your sadness naturally. Let your posture, your voice, and your facial expression show that you are sad.

Include happiness in your repertoire. Let your whole body express your joy.

When you have reclaimed the feelings you had buried and are expressing them in a way that is satisfactory to you, you are ready to choose with whom to share them. George, whose mother has Alzheimer's disease, let himself tell one of the women at work, "My mother has Alzheimer's disease, and I worry about her. I am very sad." He was embarrassed as he said this, because admitting sadness was new for him, and he told her this, too. She accepted his sadness and they talked together. Afterwards she said, "We've worked together for almost ten years, and this is the first time I've felt I really know you, George."

When you unlock your feelings and share them with others, you'll know that to feel is to be human.

It will be time then, if you like, to turn to part III and learn how to stop worrying.

CHAPTER 9

BEING HAPPY

"Whenever I'm happy, I worry that something will go wrong."

"We were having such a good time at the office party and suddenly I began to worry, because sales last month weren't quite as high as the month before. I stopped having fun."

"I got all A's for the first time in my life and right away I started to worry that I won't be able to keep it up."

"When I am out with my husband, especially when we are dancing and having a good time, I begin to worry. 'What if the house is on fire!' I worry that the kids could have left something burning on the stove. I have to telephone to check and then I'm okay for a while, until I start worrying about some other catastrophe at home, such as burglars or a falling tree."

"When I was a teenager, my father died of a heart attack. I was fishing with my friends and didn't even know about my father until I came home and saw the black wreath on our door. I remember crying and screaming and afterward feeling so guilty that I had been having a good time while my father was dying. I know it's crazy, but nowadays I often spoil my good times by worrying that someone I love may be dying."

"I have the best life I could possibly imagine, but sometimes I spoil it by worrying that my little boys may grow up to be delinquents or that there'll be a war and they'll be drafted."

Christmas is awful! I worry about how much I should spend so that I'll spend about the same amount on each person as the person spends on me. Otherwise, if I spend too much, the person may feel guilty. If I spend too little, the person will be insulted. Then I worry about what to give. I can waste hours going from store to store, worrying about not finding the right gifts. When I finally do buy something, I worry about the wrapping. Is it too impersonal to have the store wrap the gifts, even though that way they'll look nicer? I worry that my family will compare their gifts from me, and some will feel slighted. Cards are another worry! Should I keep sending cards to the people who haven't sent me a card for ten years? If I take them off the list and this time they do send a card, should I quickly send a card to reciprocate or will that look tacky? Also, I have to keep straight who gets secular cards and who gets religious ones, and sometimes I worry that they aren't secular enough or religious enough. I even worry about putting religious postage stamps, by mistake, on one of the secular cards. Christmas should be such a happy time, and I ruin it with my worries.

"I'M AFRAID TO BE TOO HAPPY"

The message "Don't be happy" is older than Solomon. It seems to be a part of every age and every culture, a magical incantation against fate, the evil eye, and a jealous

god. Through the centuries people have believed that if
you feel too good, something bad will happen. They have
believed that happiness, if seen by the gods, would bring
tragedy. War and pestilence were blamed on too much
happiness.

There are other prejudices against happiness.

"Natives," "the poor," and people of other races are
labeled "happy," and their supposed happiness is considered proof that they are ignorant and childish. Superior people are smart enough to be worried and sad.

Happy widows and widowers are suspected of "forgetting too soon."

A happy person is considered "selfish" and "insen-
sitive" to the tragedies of the world. "How can you be
happy, when there is so much trouble in your beloved
Ireland/Israel/wherever?"

No wonder people grow up believing they should be
sad and then invent worries to stifle their natural happiness.

**A women's therapy group discusses how they
learned to substitute worry for happiness. Martha's
father was ill through much of her childhood. She
says, "I know he didn't really want us to be unhappy, but we had to be quiet so that we wouldn't
disturb him. We were told that if we were noisy,
our noise could kill him. For little kids, I think the
only way to be quiet is to be sad."**

**Esther says that in her family they had lots of
fun. "However, if we got something special, like a
doll or a bicycle, we were expected to be a little
sad because there were children in the world who
didn't have any toys at all. On holidays, when the
whole family is together, Father still reminds us
that no one came to his bar mitzvah because his
family was too poor to have a party. We all cry a
few tears and hug him."**

Jo remembers her mother's chronic depression. "If we were sad, mother would comfort us. If one of us was happy, she'd say, 'Go out and play and don't bother me.'"

Karen remembers the superstitiousness of the woman who cared for her while her parents worked. When Karen would laugh, her nursemaid would say, "The bird who sings in the morning is eaten in the evening."

As the women talk about these "Don't be happy" messages, they remember other messages. Esther's Russian grandmother came up with a worry to counteract any praise. If someone told her that a grandchild had gotten all A's in school, she'd shake her head sadly and point out, "Children like him forget their families." If a child was called pretty, she'd say, "So let's hope she doesn't get tuberculosis."

The women in the group laugh as they tell all the antihappiness messages they can remember. At first they feel superior to their superstitious parents and grandparents, until they recognize that they, too, give "Don't be happy" messages to their own children. They give more love and attention when their children are sad than when they are happy. Many times they talk in front of their children about problems rather than solutions. When they worry aloud, they teach their children, by example, to be worriers.

"I'm stopping this nonsense right now," Esther says. She writes in large letters,

INDEPENDENCE AND FREEDOM DAY
This is to certify
ESTHER D.
NO LONGER BELIEVES IN WORRYING

Under that, she writes,

"My unhappiness does not make me purer, smarter, or more lovable. It doesn't keep us safe, make the crops grow, the rains fall, or the wars cease. Therefore, it is useless."

She tears the sheet off the pad and says she will hang it on the refrigerator door. The group applauds.

The women are asked to close their eyes and remember a recent happy time and to spend a few moments reliving the scene. Karen tells of laughing with an old friend about some silly things they'd done in high school. Jo teaches her grandson to turn a somersault. "I turned one first to show him how!" Esther and her husband go dancing. Martha says, "I listened to a funny tape while I was jogging, so I laughed and jogged at the same time."

Next they are asked to remember a worry. When they are remembering their worry, it is suggested that they return to their happy scene. They move back and forth between worry and happiness and recognize that they can bring on worries or banish them. They are responsible for their own thoughts and feelings.

At the close of the session, they introduce themselves as they are in their happy scene.

"I'm Esther, dancing with Simon. I'm happy and I'm still in love even after twenty-three years of marriage." She adds, "Nothing bad will happen just because I'm happy."

"This is happy Jo. She is happy and silly and kind of lovable. Yes, she's lovable. My goodness, she is also athletic for a sixty-six-year-old. She turns a mean somersault."

"I'm Martha, also athletic, also happy, and certainly silly. As I say that, I realize I'm going to make this Martha the real Martha. The sad sack is not going to be me anymore."

"I want you to meet happy Karen. People like her. And she's not a bird and she's not going to be eaten for dinner because she laughs!"

"TODAY I AM SMILING"

If you squelch your own happiness by worrying, you, too, can decide that your happiness will not bring disaster. Want to play with the idea? First, take the opposite side:

"My Tragic Fate: I must worry so that I won't be too happy, because if I am too happy, something terrible will happen somewhere in the universe, and I'll be guilty."

Say it super-tragically several times, until you want to laugh. Then repeat it with your tongue stuck on the roof of your mouth, making each word ridiculous.

When you are finished, notice that you did not worry while you were playing with the words. That proves that you can distract yourself from worrying whenever you choose.

Perhaps, like the women in the worriers' group, you would now like to experiment with finding a time and place where you are happy. It can be a scene from this morning or from fifty years ago. When you have chosen your happy scene, remind yourself that your happiness will not cause disasters to you or anyone else. Enjoy your scene and plan what you will do to continue your happiness through the day.

CHAPTER 10

SUCCEEDING

"Yesterday I got a memo from my boss, criticizing a layout I had made. That really started me worrying! I worry that I'll muff the next one, too, and be out on my ear."

"I worry about what will happen when my inheritance runs out. I can't live on my salary, and I'm years behind in child support."

"I worry about exams, because I never do well on them."

"I'm in charge of the church rummage sale, and I worry that it'll be a flop, and I'll be blamed."

"Every time I buy stock, I worry that I'll lose my shirt."

"I never say no, and then I can't possibly do all the things I promised to do, so I worry all the time."

"I CAN'T EVER WIN"

All of these worries may be reactions to "Don't be successful!" messages. Of course, almost nobody flat-out tells a child not to be successful, but the failure message gets across through groans, criticisms, and the very fact of repeated failure. The chorus of "Do we have to have Joe

on our team?" emphasizes what Joe already knows, that
he's a lousy baseball player. If you sing off-key, you'll hear
about it from the kids who are able to carry a tune. If
you can't read, it doesn't matter whether your group is
called Bluebirds or Robins or Seals or Little Angels, because you and everybody else knows that your group is
really "The First-Grade Failures."

Bill, who couldn't learn his multiplication tables, grew
up to worry about any new task. Although he was a bright
man, his childhood worries still held him back. He didn't
ask for the promotions he could easily have handled.

Some kids grit their teeth, decide they are not going
to be failures, and practice hard. Some parents help them
by hiring tutors and setting up practice times. When a
child does manage to be successful at something that was
difficult, that child ends up knowing, "I'll make it even if
it's hard at first!" That is a great thing to know about
yourself.

Other children give up. While the grade-school baseball stars play baseball every spare minute, the baseball
failures read books and program computers. When they
have to play, they stand in right field, praying that no ball
will come their way. As grown-ups, they say, "I was never
any good at sports," as if the problem were genetic and
irremediable. The kids who can't carry a tune learn to
move their lips soundlessly for the rest of their lives and
believe "I can't sing." In the same way, children who read
poorly don't spend their free time curled up with favorite
books, and so they, too, believe their lack of success
comes from an inherent failure rather than from lack of
good teaching and good practice.

For some people success is actually scary. If father
wins all the chess matches with his young son and then
stops playing as soon as his son develops the skill to win
a game, the son may come to the conclusion, "I'd better
stop winning if I want Dad to play with me." The message

is, "Don't be successful or you'll lose your father." If being a fine athlete is considered unfeminine by her high school boyfriend, a girl may become a cheerleader instead.

If the grown-ups in your family worry about money, the chances are that you, as a child, made decisions about yourself and money. You may have decided, "When I grow up, I am going to be rich, so that I'll never have to worry about money." If you stuck with that firm decision, you probably grew up to be a money-maker. Wealth can be inherited and occasionally can be acquired through luck or an extraordinary skill, but it is also acquired as the result of a decision to be wealthy, just as people who decide to be successful in other ways make their plans and carry them out.

If you said, "When I grow up, I hope something happens so that I don't have to worry about money," that may be a decision to "wait" and "hope" and thereby fail. If you had pipe dreams about money but decided early that you never get what you want or that you're not ever successful, you may have ended up like your parents. You may be angry and worried about money like your mother or sad and worried like your father. You may have decided, "None of us will ever have enough money, because we are just naturally a poor and a worrying family," as if that were the unchangeable fate of all of you.

If your mother picks on your beloved dad because he doesn't earn enough, you may have decided not to succeed in order not to show him up.

Some people think they are rebels, when in truth they are going along with the failure messages. If you are both unsuccessful and a rebel, you may have decided, "When I grow up, I'm not going to be anything like my parents, so I'm not going to worry about money. I'm not even going to think about money!" Such a decision can be disastrous, because it's almost impossible to succeed as an adult without thinking about money!

"I AM ON MY WAY!"

Perhaps you want to reverse an early decision that gets in the way of your being successful today. If you do, let yourself remember a time in your past when you decided you couldn't win. Go back to that time and tell the young you whatever fits about the truth back then.

"Hey, young one, your father criticized you because he didn't know any better. Don't give up. You can be a winner."

"There is room in a family for any number of successful people. Just because your sister was a fast learner doesn't mean you can't learn!" Explain to the child that one person's success does not have anything to do with the other person's success or failure. Each person stands on his or her own mountain. "Your success is your own, and you can succeed."

"I'm sorry schoolwork is so hard for you. Congratulations that you learned to read despite your poor eyes and lack of glasses. Today you've got the glasses and you have to study now, even though you think you're too old to do it. The success you want takes years of work."

Then say to the child from the past, "You are a success," and give some reasons: "You learned the rules of baseball," "You got a part in the school play," "You took care of your brother," "You survived a lot of sickness and pain and still found ways to earn a living." Find loving reasons why this child is a success.

When you have finished, imagine the child growing slowly until that child is you right now. Tell yourself you will not be hampered any longer by your past, either by believing you can't succeed or by wishing for a different past. It's over, and it's time to be on your way. When you've decided that it is okay for you to be successful, you'll want to claim that decision for yourself today.

THE FIRST STEP is to stop harassing yourself.

"I worry because I know I'll never get my weight down and I'm a fat slob. I can't do anything right." Separate your worry from name-calling. "I'm worried about my weight." Period.

"Damn, I'm so worried about my taxes. I've already got the final income tax extension and if I don't get my taxes in, I'll be fined. I can't do anything right." "I do lots of things right. I do need to do my taxes now."

The perpetual self-scolders live miserable lives as they delude themselves into believing that in some way, some day, all their scoldings will turn them into successful people. Not true. People don't change because they harass themselves. In fact, self-scolding takes away the confidence you need to be successful. Scolding increases misery without any positive side effects. Your first move toward success, then, is to be successful in eliminating harassment from your worry fantasies. There are many tricks for the elimination of self-harassment. Here are three:

1. Each time you begin to harass yourself, fight back against your internal tormentor. Stand up, put your hands on your hips, breathe deeply, and yell, "I am sick and tired of you! Just shut your mouth right now and leave me alone! I am not listening to you any longer." Enjoy your anger. Use all the swear words you like, shake your fist or point your finger, stamp your feet, or throw rocks at a tree. If you are in the middle of a business meeting, tell yourself that you'll have your tantrum as soon as the meeting is over.

2. As soon as you notice you are harassing yourself, apologize instead. Say aloud or silently to yourself, "I am truly sorry I spoke so impolitely to you. I wouldn't treat anyone else the way I have just treated you, and I sincerely apologize."

3. Pretend your internal harasser is a buzzing bug
   and get out an imaginary can of bug spray to
   use on it.

Use whichever of these methods you prefer, until you
are successful in taking charge of your own brain. Remember to applaud yourself for successfully reducing
self-scolding and for treating yourself kindly.

THE SECOND STEP is to recognize your successes
today. Write a Success List for this moment in your life.
Perhaps you have a happy marriage, a nicely decorated
living room, or good tomatoes growing on your sill. You
have supported yourself or made a home for whoever is
supporting you.

In one of the California valley towns there is a happy,
singing garbage collector who dresses as a bunny at Easter
and a Santa at Christmas and gives candy to the children.
Some parents have complained, saying that the pleasure
he takes in his work is making their children want to
grow up to be garbage collectors like him. Do you allow
yourself to know that there are successful garbage collectors? Or do you spoil your own successes by the kind
of rigid thinking that those parents displayed? Are you
willing to declare yourself a success right now? Only you
can determine what are successes for you.

THE THIRD STEP is to evaluate and plan for changes
you want to make in your life. You don't need worry in
order to change. You do need confidence plus an accurate
appraisal of who you are, what you can do, and what you
want to do. If you think you need help with this, find a
vocational counselor or therapist who knows how to
guide you in the direction you choose to go.

CHAPTER 11

BEING PROUD

"Every time I'm up for a promotion, I get so worried I can't eat, even though I always make top ratings and get promoted."

"I worry that I'll never be more than a vice president of the company."

"I thought I'd be okay as soon as I became a physician, but I still keep worrying and feeling like a failure.

"I worry that I am a failure, because other beauticians seem more confident. My clients like the job I do, but I still don't think I do well enough."

"I worry about being a success, and I don't even know what more I have to do to satisfy myself."

"I have low self-esteem because I'm only a housewife. I worry that my kids won't respect me when they are grown."

"I'M NEVER GOOD ENOUGH"

People who fail and people who succeed often have exactly the same worries. As you listen to worriers fret about exams they may fail or business problems they can't solve or the crops that are being destroyed by the bad weather, it's hard to tell whether they are failing in their lives or whether they are merely pretending to be failures. They may be very successful people who, instead of claiming their successes, convince themselves and others that they are always on the brink of failure. Do you have difficulty acknowledging that you are a successful person? If you do, there may be several reasons for your pretense that you're a failure.

Like the people who believe that being "too happy" courts disaster, you may believe that being "too successful" magically leads to failure. The slogan is, Pride goeth before a fall. Somewhere out there, a god or devil is waiting to zap anyone who takes pleasure in succeeding.

You may believe that the only way to keep yourself "on your toes" is to judge yourself "not quite successful yet." If you acknowledge your success, you'll "lie down on the job," become an alcoholic or a bum, and end up on Skid Row.

You may believe that other people won't like you if you are too good at what you do. This belief may have begun in grade school, when other children were jealous that you were the teacher's pet. It may also have begun at home, if your excellent grades in school were down-played in order to spare the feelings of a less successful brother or sister. Some people stop succeeding when success means unpopularity at home or at school, and others simply hide their successes behind failure worries. Unfortunately they usually end up believing in their worries rather than in their successes.

In order to believe that you are never good enough, you may grade yourself unfairly. If you are a good carpenter, do you lie to yourself by saying, "Anyone could be a carpenter?" Do you choose to stay home in order to raise your children as you want them raised, and then criticize yourself for not working outside your home? If you are a good marriage and family counselor, do you give yourself failing grades because you have a master's degree instead of a doctorate?

Another way of hiding your success is to be a High Jumper. High Jumpers are people who, after each success, yell, "Raise the bar another inch!" As children, when they brought home an honor-roll report card, they were told by their parents, "Next time get all A's." When they got all A's, their parents said, "How about A pluses?"

Sometimes this explanation doesn't fit. There are parents of High Jumpers who never suggested that the child "raise the bar another inch." They were quite happy with what the child was accomplishing, but the child wasn't. It was the children, not the parents, who "raised the bar" from their earliest school years. Do you keep raising your expectations of yourself? If you do, you may be succeeding beautifully, but you don't allow yourself to enjoy your successes.

Instead of being pleased with your successes in life, do you keep yourself worried and dissatisfied? Are you willing to change?

"OF COURSE I'M A SUCCESS!"

If you've kept yourself worried about failures that will not occur, about exams that you know you will pass, about business problems you know you can solve, how about deciding right now to enjoy your successes instead? Acknowledging and enjoying your own good work is every bit as safe as worrying and fussing and it's certainly easier on your blood pressure.

Start out your new regime by saying to yourself, "Of course I am a success," and let yourself know this is true. If you begin finding reasons to doubt your success or to worry that you can't maintain it, tell yourself,

"Of course I am a success, and my saying this will not bring on the wrath of the gods or devils."

"The fact that I acknowledge my success today will not make me end up on Skid Row."

"Now that I am acknowledging my success, I can also acknowledge the successes of my friends. I've graduated from grade school and I can find friends who like my successes, just as I like theirs."

"My success robs no one else of anything. We can each stand tall on our separate mountains." You may want to say this silently to your parents and your brothers and sisters, if it fits for you and your family.

Tell yourself that from now on you will raise the bar only on condition that you first praise yourself for what you have already done and take the time to feel good about yourself.

You are a successful realtor and you earn a good living. Fine. Praise yourself. You do not have to sell more houses, month after month, than anyone else in town or anyone else in the county or anyone else in the state. After you acknowledge your successes, you can decide if it is really important to you that you increase your yearly sales. Perhaps, in the long run, you'd be happier if you gave yourself an extra day to raise roses or lie on the couch and read mysteries. Perhaps you might enjoy giving yourself a vacation? Perhaps your family would prefer camping trips in a secondhand car instead of no vacations and high payments on a Mercedes. In order to stop raising the bar, you will have to know in your heart that you can change the rules by which you've run your life and nothing bad will happen. Fate will not strike you down for cutting your work week to forty hours or even less. You will not fall apart or become a lazy failure.

You run your household smoothly. You cook well. You have fun reupholstering your furniture and teaching the children how to make fancy picture frames. Yours is a happy family. Don't you dare raise that bar!

To let yourself enjoy your own success will not make your friends turn their backs on you. If the kids in the third grade didn't like you because you did your homework perfectly and minded the teacher, that was then. You can love your successes today and only brag to those who want you happy and successful.

Perhaps you are lacking positive strokes for all the good and successful things you have done. Today find one person who is bored with doom and gloom and would be very happy to applaud your successes. Instead of telling this person your worries, say, "I think I have done well," and give a specific example. Then ask for praise. This may be hard for you at first, but try it anyway.

If you can't think of anyone who would be willing to praise you for your successes, find someone new. With your ability to succeed, you can also succeed in finding people who will praise you.

CHAPTER 12

BEING IMPORTANT

"I worry that no one takes me seriously."
"I worry whenever I have to give a report to our women's literary club."
"I worry that my husband will leave me."

"I DON'T FEEL IMPORTANT"

People rarely come to therapy saying, "My problem is that I don't feel important." Instead, these people, who don't believe in their own importance, come in with lists of ways they should change in order to please parents, partners, or children. Even if they are acutely miserable, they'll talk only about how their behavior may be hurting others.

Georgia worries about pleasing her husband. She is a lovely woman with a full, mature body that would have been considered exquisite in almost any era except today's, when emaciation is stylish. She says she wants to lose weight for her husband. She allows him to deride her weight and complain in front of others that she eats too much. Instead of asserting herself, she agrees with whatever he says. She refuses desserts she wants and puts up with his squelching her opinions on many subjects. She does the housekeeping, even though they both have full-time careers. Her subservience tells the world that she does not consider herself important. Since her goal in therapy is to be thinner for her husband even though she knows she is not over-weight, it seems that successful therapy would in-crease her subservience.

Rachel, a single parent and graduate student, comes into therapy because she believes she is a bad mother. She says, "I don't seem to know how to make my daughter happy." Rachel worries a great deal about her daughter. Her biggest problem occurs in the evenings, when she can't get five-year-old Jodee to go to sleep. She plays with her until eight o'clock and then suggests that it is bed-time. They fight about bedtime until both are in tears, and when Jodee finally falls asleep, sometimes as late as midnight, Rachel is depressed and full of worries about what will happen to Jodee as a result of having such a bad mother. Weekends, too, are tense, because Jodee is demanding and Rachel is worried and feels guilty. She, like Georgia, enters therapy in order to make herself "better" for some-one else, in this case her daughter.

If you have difficulty believing in your own intrinsic importance, you'll understand these women. They learned early that other people are more important. How did it all begin? One way to find out is to ask, "What was dinnertime like when you were young?" The family din-ner scene often demonstrates dramatically who is im-portant and who is not.

Georgia remembers easily. "There were four of us, Mom, Pop, and my brother, who's a lot older than I am. And me." At the dinner table her father and

brother monopolize the conversation, while her
mother behaves like a servant, silently running back
and forth to the kitchen as she serves the others.
The best meat is given to the men, and her mother
rarely sits down at all. When Georgia gives an opinion, her father and brother make fun of her. She
doesn't remember anybody coming to her defense.
She is definitely not important.

How is it when you are young? If you have trouble
today believing in your own importance, what is your
dinner scene like? Let yourself become an investigative
reporter and go back in time to when you are a child.
Make the scene more real by remembering the room in
detail: the wallpaper, the table, the food in serving bowls
or on the plates. You, the reporter, are standing quietly
in the corner ready to observe this family and take notes
on their ways of relating. The family comes in and sits
down. Who sits where? Who looks at whom? Who speaks?
What do they say to each other? Who smiles and who
frowns? Observe carefully what goes on. Stay with the
memory until you have a good sense of the family dy-
namics.

When you are ready, come back to the present. What
did you learn?

Georgia uses her dinner scene to begin to assert
her importance. Because she doesn't feel capable
of defending herself in the scene, she imagines
bringing with her a powerful ally, Joan of Arc. Joan
says to the men, "Be quiet and listen to this girl. She's
a smart little kid." When the brother and father
begin to interrupt, Joan says, "I said, listen to her.
She's important. You've got a crazy idea that men
are better than women. It's not true. This little girl
is every bit as important as any man alive. Now,

Georgia, tell them again about the book you are reading." Georgia plays happily with this fantasy, sometimes acting out the part of Joan of Arc and sometimes being herself. When she feels strong enough, she sends Joan back into history and imagines herself at the table again. She says emphatically, "I am an important little girl, even if you two men don't respect me."

She weeps for that child in the past and for her mother, who continues in the same subservient role today. Then she remembers, "Hey, I really am important. I left the farm and got educated just so I wouldn't spend my life like Mom spent hers." She realizes that she has let herself drift into her mother's role in many ways since she married.

The fact that she was not respected in her childhood home was sad for little Georgia. There wasn't much she could have done about her status back then, but there is a great deal she can do about her status now. Georgia decides to stop maintaining the pattern she learned in childhood. After defending herself successfully in the fantasized dinner scene, she practices being her own defender in her present home. For her it is one step at a time. She begins by giving herself positive messages and fighting back silently against the negative ones from her husband. It takes her several months to develop enough self-esteem to tell her husband that she is not going to accept insults about her weight or anything else for that matter. When he doesn't change, it takes her another year to leave him. During that year she practices being important with friends and with colleagues at work. She receives a raise, which she uses to hire household help.

Today she says, "When I read fairy tales as a child, I believed that 'happily ever after' had to mean being married. Now I live alone. Whatever I choose in the future, I will not be a victim, and for me that is living "happily ever after."

When Rachel realizes that she lacks self-importance, she joins an assertiveness-training group. In the group she becomes aware that she has the right to demand that the day care personnel stop forcing Jodee to take long afternoon naps. With group support she practices a confrontation with the day care administrator about naps. The members critique her performance and wish her well as she sets out to talk to the administrator. At the next session she is giggling like a happy kid. "A piece of cake! The administrator agrees with me. I'm still amazed."

Even more amazing to her is the change that is evolving in her relationship with Jodee. In the evenings she and Jodee play together until bedtime, when she tucks Jodee in, kisses her good night, and tells her she may play with her dolls in bed or she may go to sleep. She may not bother Rachel, because this is Rachel's study time. After a remarkably few skirmishes, Jodee settles down.

Rachel has allowed herself to be important instead of guilty, and her little girl seems reassured by these changes.

Some people feel important at home, but leave their importance behind when they step out the front door. They don't consider themselves important in the neighborhood or at work. They plague themselves with worries about what the others will think and keep themselves from speaking out by believing, "Everyone else has already thought of this," or "If I suggest that, someone will put me down." They volunteer to be members of clean-up committees instead of being officers of their organizations.

Perhaps as children they didn't come from "important families." Perhaps they spent their childhoods being "tag-alongs" behind older siblings, instead of finding their own friends. Whatever the individual reasons for being unimportant in the past, all people can change in the present.

"OF COURSE I AM IMPORTANT"

Do you have difficulty being important? If it fits for you, use your fantasy of your family dinner to begin to change yourself. This time, when you go back to the family dinner table, be yourself instead of an investigative reporter. Take an ally with you if you like or assert your importance on your own. Either way is fine, so long as you get the message across: "I am important. My thoughts are important, my feelings are important, and my actions are important." Look at each one of them as you say this. Recognize that all people have a right to their own importance. Tell the family again, "I am important," and let yourself know the truth of that statement, whether or not everyone in the family agrees with you.

Now that you have asserted your importance, act it out in fantasy. Seat yourself again at the dinner table and tell the family something interesting that you did. "I learned to read six new words." "I jumped off the swing farther than anyone else." "I saw a butterfly." Barge right into the conversation and say loudly what you did. If, in your imagination, anyone downgrades what you say or disputes your importance, tell that person firmly, "You have a problem. You think dinnertime is like a King of the Mountain contest. When I tell about me, you try to push me down, so that only you are important. That's not necessary. We are all important at this table, and that includes you and me." Perhaps, in your fantasy, they listen to you and perhaps they don't. It doesn't matter, because your importance depends on your own decision. Say it again, "I'm important."

Be your adult self and applaud the young you at the dinner table. That child is important and the child's importance does not rely on other people's approval. Now imagine yourself at your dinner table today, being important and making time for others to be important, too.

Go to your place of work and say to yourself, "I am important here, too." Decide on a suggestion you will make at work, and do not let your old worries get in your way. Instead, figure out whether your idea is a good one. You are important enough to know the difference between a suggestion made because it will be helpful and a suggestion made in order to receive a putdown. To learn to be important, you'll want to begin with suggestions that will bring you positive recognition. You can criticize and take minority positions later, after you are comfortable with asserting yourself.

The next time you notice that you are making up a worry that discounts your importance, change the ending. For example:

"I am sitting on the couch, reading a novel, and suddenly I am worrying about having to give a report at work. I may forget what to say."

Make the ending of your worry positive.

"I forget what to say, so I ask, 'Have you followed me so far? Any questions?' Then, if I still don't remember, I ask, 'Where was I, anyway?' And I feel okay with myself."

You do not have to be perfect to be important. You can mispronounce a word or forget what you wanted to say. You can ask your audience, "Questions, anyone?" That acknowledges their importance and gives you time to collect your thoughts.

Fantasize not knowing an answer to a question. Say, "I don't know," and continue happily with your talk. Imagine yourself and others sharing importance without being perfect.

Perhaps your worry is that someone will drop in on you when your house is a bit messy. Instead of rushing to make it perfect, hear yourself say, "Hi, glad to see you. Come on in. I was just about to clean this house, but it's so much more fun to visit with you." Or, "Thanks for stopping by, but I'm about to clean house, so come another time. Perhaps next Tuesday afternoon?"

Whenever you change your worry fantasies and assert your own importance, be sure you congratulate yourself. It isn't easy to change lifelong patterns, and you deserve praise for whatever changes you are making. Have you a friend you are willing to share your changes with? That's another way to claim your importance.

CHAPTER 13

BELONGING

"I worry about what will happen when my children are grown. I adore them! They are darling little girls and they look exactly like my wife, who is Japanese. We are a very close, loving family, and yet I worry that I'll end up the outsider. I worry that my wife and daughters will go live in Japan, even though I know they won't. My girls don't speak Japanese and, in fact, I am the only one in the family who would want to live in Japan."

"I worry that I won't wear the right outfit. I worry that if I wear a dress, the others will wear slacks. I want to be dressed like everyone else."

"I worry about not fitting in at work."

"I want to join the Elks, but I worry about whether they'd want me."

"I'M AN OUTSIDER"

People who feel unimportant may or may not be estranged from others. The ones who believe they don't belong feel estranged rather than unimportant. They are outsiders, looking at their family or society from a distance. They have a hard time saying, "Include me, too!"

If your worries are about being an outsider, you may have decided when you were just a child that you didn't fit in. Perhaps yours was the only Jewish family in town. Perhaps your family belonged in the community, but you were labeled "the shy one," and the label stuck. Perhaps you were "different," because you were brighter than the other kids or because you lived on an isolated farm and had no time for play after school.

Jan came into therapy because she believed she had never belonged anywhere. Her therapist asks when she first felt this way. Jan said, "Second grade." She'd been a star pupil, a teacher's pet, and her memory is that she is somehow different from everyone else. She is asked to close her eyes and in fantasy, to revisit her grade school in order to find out more about her isolation then. In her fantasy she is sitting on a bench in the playground reading a book. The other children are jumping rope, playing jacks, throwing balls, and chasing one another. She is asked, "What do you feel?" "Well, I feel superior. I'm reading a book they can't even read. Honestly, I'm lonely. So very lonely."

Her therapist empathizes with that very lonely child and then asks Jan to notice, in her imagination, if there are any other children sitting on the bench. She sees two others, one kicking the toes of her shoes in the sand and one staring across the playground. She even remembers their names, because they were always sitting there, too. "Mary Lou and Linda. They don't have anyone to play with, either."

"So, how about you doing something different today? How about asking Mary Lou and Linda if they want to play jacks with you?"

"I'm no good at jacks."

"Of course. That's because you never practice. All you do is read and feel lonely."

Jan laughs. "How did you know?"

"A lot of little kids don't learn how to belong, even though they are very smart at learning how to read, so they read more and more, when they should be practicing how to belong. Take your jacks over to Mary Lou and Linda and ask them if they want to play. Imagine the three of you playing and imagine yourself smiling and laughing."

Jan enjoys the fantasy. She thinks up several other ways that she, as a child, can belong to a group. After practicing childhood belonging during the therapy hour, she and her therapist discuss how she can practice belonging in her present life. For starters, she decides to stop envying popular, busy women and look for the Mary Lous and Lindas, who can also be interesting.

The easiest way to belong is to find a group that needs you. These groups exist in every community and all anyone has to do is volunteer to help out. Jan finds a small church group that was delighted to have a new member.

Another lonely woman, Laura, is a retired executive secretary. Her retirement dream was to move to Santa Barbara, California, where she could walk by the ocean and enjoy the mild climate. When her dream comes true, it feels more like a nightmare. She is growing deaf, and is isolated, and severely depressed. At that point her physician refers her to a therapy group. In group she says that she doesn't belong there, because she is too old and too deaf, and her problems are physical rather than psychological. She does agree to keep coming to the sessions and makes an important commitment to herself and the group that she will not kill herself no matter how depressed she becomes. As she works in group, she begins to realize that she has never felt she belonged and that her job had taken the place of any warm emotional ties. That was why she had so easily moved from the Midwest to Santa Barbara. She becomes a little less depressed, smiles occasionally, and begins to accept the fact that she is an important, loved member of this group. Outside of the therapy group, she remains an isolated woman.

One day a group member tells her how much a local political group needs someone with secretarial ability. Laura is pushed to volunteer. At the second meeting she attends, she is made editor of their local newsletter. She keeps that job for over fifteen years.

At her eightieth birthday party, she tells her political friends, "My goodness, I am too busy to die, so you'll probably have to do this again when I'm ninety!" She is obviously happy and, just as obviously, she belongs.

"MAKE ROOM FOR ME"

If you want to learn the art of belonging, you might start with your family. Do you belong there? If not, what do you want to do about it? You can't change them against their will, but you can change yourself. The first step is to stop being one of the waiting folks of the world. These are the people who hang around, waiting and hoping that the others will throw them a crumb of friendship. Are you willing to get what you want instead of waiting for a handout? What you want is to belong. There are rules that will work in almost any group and in most families:

- Start giving simple compliments. "You look pretty in that blue dress." "I've always liked your smile." "I agree with what you are saying." "Tell me more about your job. I don't know much about it, and I'd like to." Do not overcomplicate and never mix negatives into your compliments. Don't say, "You look much prettier in that blue dress than in your green one." Don't say, "I like your smile, but your teeth would be whiter if you'd stop smoking."

- Invite family members to do things with you that you know they like to do. "I'll row the boat if I can go fishing with you." "You like adventure movies, and this one is supposed to be great. Let me treat us to it."

- Do not attempt to change any of them, because attempting to change them means that you do not accept them the way they are, and that fact alone can cause estrangement.

- Don't keep score. What difference does it make if you do the inviting or if they do? Laura's political group contained people who worked actively in the group and people who did nothing except come to meetings. Families are the same.

If you do all of the above and still feel like an outsider in your family, you may choose to stop putting your efforts into your family and instead look for other groups to join. The same rules apply outside the family. Like Jan in grade school, you might look for friends who are also "sitting on the bench."

Join groups that fit your interests. You can hike with nature-study groups, be a member of the local romance writers' club, or find the association of Oz book buffs. Offer your services to any group that needs help. Are you willing to do what Laura did, find a way to be useful to others?

If none of this seems right for you, join a psychotherapy group and learn how to belong.

You can do for you what Jan and Laura did for themselves. Have a fun, productive time belonging!

CHAPTER 14

PLAYING

"I am always worrying about my sister. She doesn't take good care of herself, and I have to end up doing things for her."

"My son is in medical school and doing very well. I worry that he isn't eating properly and that he'll get run down and catch some disease from a patient. When I can't take care of him, I worry about him."

"Sometimes I think I worry about everyone in the world except myself!"

"I work 80 hours a week. I'd like to take it easy, but I worry about all the things I have to do."

"I'd like to dance, but I worry that I'll look awkward."

"A month ago I had two glasses of wine at a party and I got silly. Ever since, I've worried about what everyone must think of me!"

"I NEVER WAS A KID"

Do your worries keep you from taking time off and having fun? If you find yourself being overly responsible, per-fectionistic, and hardworking, you've probably learned to

set very high goals, never to say no, and to worry whenever you aren't working. Perhaps you went to work while
you were still in grade school and have been working
ever since.

In the early days of the hippies there was a young
woman named Julie who certainly didn't believe
in working too hard. She played the guitar, took a
few classes, and was looking for a part-time job.
She was also in a therapy group. One day her new
boss telephoned Julie's therapist. "Are you Julie's
therapist?" It was explained to him that such information is never given out.

"Well, let me tell you why I am calling. My name
is Richard Jones. I run a music store, and I'd ad-
vertised for a salesperson. This beautiful young
woman, Julie, came in to apply for the job. When
I told her how much I was willing to pay per hour,
she added it up and said, 'Oh, good, I'd only have
to work eighteen hours a week at that salary to pay
my bills. I was afraid I'd have to work twenty-four
hours to earn the money I need.' Well, let me tell
you, I was so flabbergasted, I hired her on the spot.
She only wanted to work the minimum! I'd never
met anyone quite like her before."

He then told his story. When he was ten years
old, he began helping his father tune pianos. He
had perfect pitch and was proud of all the compliments he received for being a piano tuner at such
a young age. He kept on working every day after
school and all day on Saturdays and gave his father
the money he made. When he finished school, he
and his father worked together full-time. He sold,
repaired, and tuned instruments, and when his
father died, he took over the business. He kept his
store open seven days a week and tuned pianos
evenings. Now he was phoning for an appointment.

"I never thought of seeing a psychotherapist before, but if you can make me just a little bit like Julie, it will be worth the money." He hoped the therapist would tune him as he had tuned pianos. "I want to be changed so that I can take time off and sit on the beach, like Julie does, and do absolutely nothing for an entire afternoon."

Therapists are always delighted to find clients like Richard. The Julies of the world love therapy but don't have much incentive to change, and they often don't pay their bills. The personal changes they need may involve work and goal setting and sticking it out even when the job is boring or difficult and they aren't interested in working hard. Clients like Richard already work hard, so therapists can offer them delightful goals, such as vacations and friendships and a whole afternoon sitting on the beach. Naturally they appreciate their therapists and always pay their bills.

Are you a hardworking loner like Richard? If so, you are probably far ahead in life. You learned early to sacrifice your childhood in the pursuit of good grades and high achievement. Other people may complain that they never had the opportunity to become a doctor or a lawyer or a businessman, but you know that you made that opportunity for yourself. You learned how to take care of yourself at an early age. Now if you choose to change, your hardworking years will have paid off. You have the time now to learn to give to yourself. You'll learn to be easier on yourself, to like yourself better, and to give yourself freedom to have fun. You can even afford to buy your own skis and snorkeling equipment and to go on holidays. That's what Richard did. He celebrated his changes by giving himself his first vacation, a week in Tahiti. His next step was finding someone to play with.

Unfortunately the hardworking loners often have problems with intimacy. One of their reasons for working

so hard is to avoid the pain of not belonging and not
being close. When you have given yourself permission to
play, your next goal may be giving yourself permission
to love and be close. That, too, is an exciting quest.

Another group of people who missed out on childhood are the young caretakers of the world. Did you have
to grow up fast in order to take care of others? Were you
the oldest in your family and therefore a caretaker from
the time you were practically a baby yourself? Perhaps
you are the child of alcoholics or chronically ill parents,
so you shouldered the family responsibilities. Unlike the
workaholic loner, you did learn to love, but you have
love and caretaking all mixed together. Want to separate
them?

If so, you need to believe firmly that others have the
same obligations you have. Like you, other adults are
responsible for themselves. Can you believe that? You
don't have to take care of little brothers and sisters or
little sons and daughters forever. Your fifty-year-old little
brother and your twenty-one-year-old daughter have
been helped by you long enough. It's your turn now.

It isn't always easy to let go of the people you've cared
for. Some of them are very insistent that they need you.
Are you willing to let them sink, if that is their choice?
That is an important question that only you can answer.

Think about your caretaking when you were a child.
Were you ever really successful in keeping your parents
from fighting, drinking, divorcing? How would they have
been different if you had never existed? Probably they'd
have been exactly as they were. All your efforts to help
them or change them were really in vain.

"IT'S NOT TOO LATE FOR
A HAPPY CHILDHOOD"

Put yourself briefly into a family scene in which you were trying to help. Perhaps your parents are quarreling, perhaps your mother is crying and not caring for the little ones. Perhaps you are washing clothes at an age when other children are playing baseball. In your imagination hear yourself tell them, "I'm only a kid. Kids are supposed to play, and I am going out to play." Imagine leaving them to fight, drink, diaper the babies, or plow the fields. Notice that they are not getting along well without you, but they didn't get along well in life with your assistance, either. They managed in their own way before you were born and after you left home, so they didn't really need you as much as you thought. Imagine yourself guilt-free, as you skip out of the house to join the other kids playing baseball or flying kites.

Here is another exercise to help you give up being responsible for those who don't really need you. Imagine that you are sitting in front of a giant switchboard, working overtime to keep all the lines plugged in properly. You are caring for everyone. Move your hands faster and faster as you keep your son plugged in to studying, your daughter plugged in to her marriage, the neighbors plugged in to lawn watering, the altar guild plugged in to ironing vestments. Move your hands faster and faster, as if the fate of the universe is in your hands. Keep plugging in the lines, and as you plug them in, say aloud, "I am responsible for you, to be sure you do what you should." Say it to each person, as you work faster and faster, until you are ready to give up.

Ready? Tell your imaginary, giant switchboard, "I'm resigning from this job," and let the lines fall to the carpet.

As you walk around the switchboard, take a good look at it. Notice that there are no wires running to the people whom you've been trying to keep plugged in. All the wires are lying helter-skelter on the carpet. Your switchboard is a phony. Not one of the lines was really connected to anyone. You only imagined that you were directly connected to the success or failure of others. Give the phony lines a kick and then imagine yourself walking away from that switchboard forever.

If you are working so many hours each week that you are too tired to play, ask yourself if this is necessary. Perhaps it is, if it is important to you to own an expensive home or get your business started well. If it is necessary now, how can you maintain your schedule and still fit in pleasurable activities? Check your calendar carefully to see what changes you can make. Perhaps there are little things you can change. You might hire a teenager to wash your car or take the children to the park one afternoon a week. If you are already overworking, postpone volunteer work until you've reached a time in your life when you can cut back. Be inventive on your own behalf.

For the rest of the week, whether you are a caretaker or a hardworking loner, find activities for yourself that are fun. Take a slow walk and admire the flowers you see. Have a bubble bath. Take fifteen minutes to read a funny book at a time when you are usually working. When you get a phone call from someone asking your help or advice, let yourself say, "Wow, that is a problem." "My goodness, I do wonder how you'll solve that." "Hey, be sure to let me know how you handle it." "Sorry, I can't help."

Find a friend who laughs a lot.

CHAPTER 15

BEING DIFFERENT

"My biggest worry is a stupid one, 'Do I look all right?' I worry about what is 'all right.' Should I try to be sophisticated or plain or sexy or charming? I ask my friends what makeup I should use, and I've hired a wardrobe consultant, and I still don't like the way I am."

"I'm a teacher and I love teaching children, but I was supposed to have been a physicist. I keep worrying that my parents are disappointed in me. And I worry that someday I may regret that I became a teacher."

"I worry that I'm not the way a man should be. I look feminine."

"THERE'S SOMETHING WRONG WITH ME"

Some people go through life believing that they were "born wrong." They say to themselves, "There's always been something wrong about me." Sometimes this belief is the result of parental disappointment in a child.

Perhaps you are the only son of a football coach and you were not good at sports. Perhaps you were supposed to be a beautiful baby doll and you were a plain little girl who was good at climbing trees. Perhaps you are the third daughter in a family that yearns for sons.

Sometimes society, rather than parents, tells a child, in effect, "You are not okay the way you are."

Almost all psychological tests of gender identity show that about 60 to 70 percent of little boys are a certain way and 60 to 70 percent of little girls are another way. These tests are used to prove that differences exist. Most little boys supposedly build towers with blocks and most little girls build nests. More little boys than little girls are tough, don't cry, and want to be in Little League, but 30 to 40 percent do not test like the majority. That is a tremendous number.

Think about these millions of children. Instead of using percentages to prove that boys and girls are different in their block building or their baseball throwing, it would be kinder to acknowledge that millions of perfectly healthy children do not fit stereotypes. What happens to the little boys who build the nests, who are not tough, who do cry, who hate baseball? What about their sisters who are the opposite? Some of them do just fine, because they come from families that applaud their choices and like them just the way they are. Some of them, however, are derided at home or at school and end up secretly believing that there is "something wrong with me."

At least 10 percent of all boys, some of whom built towers and some of whom did not, some of whom liked Little League and some of whom did not, grow up to be men who love men. At least 10 percent of all girls, baseball players and homemakers both, grow up to be women who love women. Society tells them, "Don't be what you are."

If you are a person whose interests, occupation, or patterns of loving do not fit so-called norms, are you willing to love yourself just the same? Fortunately nowadays there are lots of male knitters and jelly makers, female carpenters and judges, so the stereotypes are becoming less rigid. If your lover is of your own sex, there are also millions of other gays and lesbians who are out of the closet, plus a growing number of heterosexuals who are supporting your choice.

Some people are solidly "in the majority" all through life and still don't feel right about themselves. Did you believe that if only you were somehow different, you'd be acceptable, but you didn't know quite what to change? Usually this problem has nothing whatsoever to do with the individual child. The child was fine, but was raised by parents who, because of their own problems, didn't know how to like children of any kind.

"I'M OKAY THE WAY I AM"

You have a right to love and respect yourself as you are. Begin at the beginning.

Imagine that you are visiting a big-city hospital. You ask directions to the nursery, and a nurse points the way. The nursery has a large plate-glass window and behind the window are twelve bassinets, each holding a newborn baby. Look at them. Some of the babies are red and wrinkled, some are slightly yellowish or slightly blue or splotchy white, and some are various shades of tan and brown. Some are almost bald and some have lots of hair. Some are screeching and some are sleeping. If you were going to be picky, you'd probably admit that none of them are as cute as kittens. If you are a baby-lover, you know that each baby is unique, new, beautiful, and infinitely lovable.

Look at the babies and decide which one is you, then go into the nursery and pick yourself up. Say to this newborn who is you, "I'm learning to love you just the way you are." "There is nothing wrong with you." "You are like all the other babies, and I love you." You might want to practice this fantasy until you believe every word of it.

Get a full-length mirror and learn to love what you see.

CHAPTER 16

WANTING AND RECEIVING

"Christmases and birthdays are worrisome times. I worry about the presents I buy and I worry that my family will get me things I can't use and then be mad when I return their presents."

"I worry that everyone will forget my birthday."

"I worry that I'll never get married just because I want it so much."

"I don't want anything. That way I don't have to worry about not getting anything. I worry about the world or my health or something else instead."

"I DON'T GET WHAT I WANT"

There are many different ways to teach people not to ask for what they want.

When Jean is a little girl, she occasionally visits her great-great aunt, who sits very straight with her old hands folded in her lap and stares at Jean. Jean sits very straight on the couch, trying not to look too hard at the candy dish and also trying to look at it hard enough to remind her great-great aunt that there is candy in the dish. Jean is never supposed to ask for candy, because it isn't polite. You are supposed to wait and hope someone guesses. Jean has always wondered why grown-ups invent such crazy rules.

If her great-great aunt doesn't want to share her candy, wouldn't she hide it, the way Jean hides her own after Halloween? Either she'd hide it or she'd be like awful Great-grandmother Burkhardt, who only shares candy that no one would want, called hoarhound. Great-great Aunt has good chocolates right there in the dish where everyone can see them, except perhaps Great-great Aunt, who is getting blind and also forgetful. Wouldn't Jean be doing her a favor to say, "Are you going to give me some chocolates?"

Jean decides that when she grows up, she'll have enough candy for everyone and nobody will have to wait politely. They won't even have to ask. All they'll have to do is grab.

Unfortunately, however, when Jean grows up, she inherits diabetes, so about the time she could always have enough candy, she can't eat it.

The moral is, Gather ye chocolates while ye may, for time it is a flying, which means, For goodness' sake, ask for what you want while you can still have it!

There are six basic rules for not getting what you want:

1. Don't know what you want.
2. Know what you want, but don't give it to yourself.

3. Know what you want, but don't tell anybody who would give it to you.
4. Know what you want, and only tell the ones who won't give it to you.
5. Want only what no one can give you.
6. Get what you want, but don't feel satisfied.

If it seems to you that you don't get what you want, check out whether any of these rules apply to you.

DON'T KNOW WHAT YOU WANT

Sometimes people don't know what they want, because they found wanting too dangerous when they were children. Some children receive terrible messages against wanting:

> A man was letting his baby son ride on the railing of the moving sidewalk at the San Francisco airport. He was bouncing him and chanting, "A-gallop, A-gallop, A-gallop," while the baby squealed with delight. His little girl, only about a year older than the baby, raised her arms and said, "Me, too?" The father backhanded, as if to slap her, and she ducked silently and didn't ask again. The father continued playing horse with the baby. That little girl may find it is safest never to want.

Some people don't know their own wants because they were not supposed to think for themselves:

When Susie said, "I want the red dress," her mother
would buy her the blue one and tell Susie that the
blue dress was the one she really wanted. Susie
grew up very confused. When she enters therapy
and her therapist asks, "What do you want to accomplish here?" Susie doesn't know. She spends a
considerable amount of time and money trying to
figure out what the therapist wants for her. Finally
she decides that her major "want" is to learn her
own desires. She starts with the red dress.

She imagines she is the young Susie in the department store, talking to her mother. "I know that
you like the blue dress best. I like the red dress.
Maybe it isn't made of good enough material, maybe
it's too fancy for school. Maybe it isn't the dress
you are going to buy me. None of that matters.
What matters is that I know my own mind. I want
the red dress because that is the one I like!" She
continues, "When I grow up, I will know what I
want."

After this therapy session, she practices knowing her own wants, beginning with simple things
that she can give herself. "After work tonight I want
to drive out of town to see the sunset." "I want the
sweater I bought myself. I bought it because I
wanted it, not just because it was on sale. I like the
color, whether mother or anyone else likes it or
not." She learns to congratulate herself for knowing
her own mind, rather than doubting herself or has-
sling herself over her decisions. Her next self-
chosen task is to tell others what she wants and to
ask them to give to her. She finds out that some
will and some won't, and that that is okay. She is
overjoyed by the fact that she is asking, and for the
first time she feels like a real person rather than a
shadow of someone else.

Adults who don't know what they want often feel stuck, confused, and frustrated. They wonder when it will be their turn in life.

KNOW WHAT YOU WANT BUT DON'T GIVE IT TO YOURSELF

Perhaps you use worries to keep yourself from wanting. Each time you want a power saw, you may start to worry about the world financial situation. Or do you worry about the poor little children in Bangladesh rather than notice that you want a new toaster and two new friends?

Giving to yourself can be an adventure, if you are willing to make it that. Tell yourself that giving to yourself will not make you stupid or selfish. You won't go hog-wild because you are learning to care well for yourself. If it's an issue for you, you can learn to be both self-giving and practical. Make a budget that includes a sum for your Want List. That way you can have the fun of indulging yourself without worrying about going broke. And don't forget that there are wants that cost no money. You may want to give yourself a trip to the library on Saturday, instead of making Saturdays a grueling clean-up day. It is important that you learn to give to yourself without regrets or worry later.

KNOW WHAT YOU WANT BUT DON'T TELL ANYONE WHO WOULD GIVE IT TO YOU

What do you do about your birthday? Perhaps you don't even remind your children or your lover that your birthday is coming, because, you tell yourself, birthdays are no big deal. Or do you not tell and then worry that they will forget, which any normally preoccupied person is bound to do? If you expect them to remember, you are confusing love and memory. If you expect them to know what you want without telling them, you are confusing love with clairvoyance.

Do you say, "Oh, get me anything," and then not like your presents? Do you always receive lingerie, which you hate, because you don't let them know what will really please you? Have you fifty ties that you will never wear, because everyone celebrates Father's Day by giving you a new tie? How about telling them to put the money together and get you what you really want?

Learning to ask for what you want takes practice and begins with small steps. The payoff is increased self-respect as well as good presents.

If you want to share the cooking in your home, say so. If you want someone else to take out the garbage on alternate nights, tell that person what you want. If you like little surprise gifts, tell your lover that, and also tell your lover where he or she can purchase the type of surprises that please you. Give good instructions. Then if you find you are not getting positive action in response to reasonable requests, you may want to study some books on being affirmative so that you can improve the way you ask. Or you may want to find people who are more giving and put them in your life.

KNOW WHAT YOU WANT AND ONLY TELL THE ONES WHO WON'T GIVE IT TO YOU

Do you tell your mother that for your birthday you want cash for new jeans, when you know she won't give money and that she hates jeans? You could just as easily ask her to buy your sweaters or your books and you buy your own jeans, if you are willing to get what you want rather than not get it and be angry.

WANT ONLY WHAT NO ONE CAN GIVE YOU

Do you say, "Well, the only thing I really want is ten years off my age" or "A trip around the world"? If you do that, you deny the giver the joy of giving, just as you deny yourself the joy of receiving.

GET WHAT YOU WANT, BUT DON'T FEEL SATISFIED

There are many ways to remain dissatisfied after receiving. One way is to blemish the gift.

Raymond learned to be dissatisfied when he was little more than a baby. He had four doting grandparents, two doting parents, and assorted doting uncles and aunts, all of whom loved giving him presents. One day his grandmother said, "We're going to make cookies," and she showed him all the new animal cookie cutters she had bought just for cookie making with him. He looked at them, loved them, and excitedly said his favorite word, "Wow!" Then he said, "No cow." His grandmother was delighted and raced to tell his grandfather, "That child is so smart, he noticed right away that there wasn't a cow." both of them kissed him and hugged him, and grandfather made a tin cookie-cutter cow just for Raymond. Everyone in the family bragged, "He is so smart! Barely two years old, and he notices there's no cow."

He was, in truth, smart enough to recognize what he was supposed to do in order to please all his relatives. The next time he was given something, a doll, he said, "No toes," and again they cheered. For Christmas he got a truck and he said, "No tractor," and they cheered again. From then on, he scarcely noticed what he got because he was so busy discovering what he didn't get. By the time he was three, the relatives asked each other, "What is wrong with that child? He's never satisfied!" Finally one of them remembered how it all began, with the cow. They agreed that from then on they would hug and kiss him when he was satisfied and ignore him when he told them what was missing. In a very few months he had forgotten to look for ways of being dissatisfied. By being smart, his relatives saved Raymond a lot of future grief.

Do you act like the little boy with the cookie cutters? If you recognize that pattern in yourself, you can use this same behavior modification on yourself. Praise yourself for being satisfied and ignore your ways of blemishing the things you receive.

Some people are unhappy when they receive, because they expected too much from the gift, like a person who goes to a plastic surgeon for a nose job and thinks the new nose will bring instant lovers, promotions, and eternal good feelings. Actually a nose job is simply a new and nicer nose, which can be appreciated for itself.

Another way to spoil your happiness is by worrying instead of enjoying the gifts you've been given. When you finally get the power saw or dishwasher you wanted, do you begin to worry that you spent too much? If so, you may have come from a family that believes there is something sinful or selfish in receiving. They are wrong.

Caretakers of the world worry that the giver didn't really want to give or couldn't afford the gift. Gloria, Jean's mother, always worried about people doing too much for her.

> Once, when she was an old lady, she had lunch with grown-up Jean and Jean's friend. The friend paid the bill. They'd had a fine, happy time until then. Gloria offered to pay her share, and when the friend refused, she began to worry. "Are you sure you can afford it, dear?" The woman tried to reassure her. Gloria said, "I feel so guilty. If I had known you were paying, the least I could have done was order hamburger instead of crab!"

Do you let people decide for themselves whether they can afford to buy you crab?

Sometimes, of course, you don't get your wants met even though you follow all the rules. You state your wants clearly to the right people at the right time, and nothing happens. You can ask again or get it for yourself, and sometimes you'll do without.

RULES FOR SUCCESSFUL WANTING

The rules for successful wanting are:

1. Know what you want.
2. Give to yourself.
3. Ask for what you want from those who will give to you.

4. Enjoy receiving.
5. Accept not receiving, and keep on wanting, giving, asking, and enjoying.

Let yourself know, "Life is a gift to be received with joy." Each gift that you are given or that you get for yourself can be received in the same spirit.

CHAPTER 17

BEING INTIMATE

"Whenever I fall in love with someone, I know he'll eventually get tired of me, so I break off with him before he has a chance to break off with me. That way, I'm never deserted."

"Whenever I fall in love, I start to notice little things wrong with her, and I worry that I might get trapped into a relationship with someone I'll end up not liking at all."

"I worry about AIDS, so I don't date much."

"I worry that I'll never get married again, because I'm already thirty-five and I have two kids."

"I don't dare advertise for a date, because I'd worry too much that the person who answers the ad will be a murderer. Look at how many murders are reported every day in the newspaper."

"I worry that I'll be crowded out of my own home by someone else's things."

"I'M NOT LOVABLE, AND YOU'RE NOT TRUSTABLE"

All of these people believe they want intimacy, want lovers or husbands or wives, and yet they use their worries to remain alone. At the first glorious hint of love, they create worries instead. When they could have love and fun in the present, they write worry stories about a future of disenchantment, abandonment, loneliness, and even murder. They use worry about the future to keep from being loved in the present, without realizing that their loneliness is a result of the worries they write in their heads.

Gary worries that his lover will find out he is not interesting enough and leave him, so Gary finds an excuse to leave instead. Gary is alone, just as he predicted he would be. Josie finds minor faults with her lover and enlarges them into horrendous worries of future disenchantment. She nags him to change, until he does leave her. Her predictions come true. She is still alone and unmarried.

Gary remembers his final worry before leaving Chris. They are at a theater, holding hands as they watch a movie. Suddenly Gary begins to worry, "What if Chris is tired of me?" No longer hearing the movie or sensing Chris's hand in his, Gary elaborates on his worry, until he is even imagining what Chris would say on walking out the door for the last time. In therapy Gary wonders why he does this. His therapist asks, "Who deserted you when you were little?" At first he believes that he's never been deserted. He comes from a very correct, unemotional family, who watches the evening news while eating dinner and are rarely in the same room together at any other time. His parents work long hours, so in a sense are absent, but they never desert him. And then he remembers: When he is very little, he has a housekeeper who loves him.

He sobs, recalling how this woman sang to him as she rocked him. One day she is gone and another woman takes her place.

Gary's family never explains what happened to her except that "She went back to Ireland." There is no one to help him mourn. In therapy he lets himself visualize the woman, say good-bye, and mourn his real loss. Then he mourns the loss of Chris, who is now with someone else. He feels very sad, and infinitely relieved. He says, "I think I've solved an important puzzle in my life. I always did have a shadowy memory that I was once different, more warm and trusting." He continues in therapy in order to keep from sabotaging himself as he seeks to trust and love. Later in his therapy he recognizes that the first desertion that affected him occurred long before he was born. His mother's mother and father died when she was a child, and that tragedy may well have caused her lack of intimacy with her own son. He believes that his family's life stance is "Don't love too much or you'll get hurt."

Josie is the oldest child of alcoholics. In childhood she learns to expect the worst, because it usually happens. She also learns to be bossy as she tries hard to keep her family functioning and to take care of her little brothers. It is an impossible task for a child. Her childhood hope is to get her parents to stop drinking. In therapy she learns to take her drunken father's face off the men in her life, so that she can enjoy men rather than try to reform them. Gradually, with the help of her therapist and a particularly understanding new lover, she learns to permit herself the intimacy she's always wanted.

Michelle only dates men with a history of unfaithfulness. When she starts psychotherapy, she is dating a man who is unfaithful to her, just as her ex-husband had been. She wants very much to be married and wonders if she'll ever meet anyone who is willing to marry a divorced woman with two children. Her therapist focuses on Michelle's lack of self-esteem. One day, as she enters the therapist's office, Michelle is humming an old song, "Secondhand Rose." When the therapist comments on it, Michelle says that her mother sang it to her when she was a child. Michelle denies that it could be meaningful. A few weeks later she comes to her therapy session in a rage. "That damned song! Of course, it fits! It's the story of my life!" She pounds a few pillows, yells at herself, her mother, and fate, and then says quite seriously, "I am not going to have a secondhand life."

At age thirty-five she gives up loving other people's lovers. She moves to the West Coast to make a "fresh start," gets a job, buys herself three attractive outfits that mix and match into a dozen combinations, and sets out to find a husband. From the chamber of commerce she receives a list of all the organizations in the area and joins ones that are at least 50 percent male: Downtown Democrats, Sierra Club, a tennis club, and a computer club. She tells her children, "I'm looking for a husband, and that means I won't be with you every evening, the way I used to be. But I'll be settled down soon, so hang in there." Each time she meets a man, she checks out whether he fits her basic requirements: free to marry now, good job, and compatible religious and political beliefs. Her previous experience, coupled with her new self-esteem, make it easy for her to predict who is seriously interested in marriage. She drops those who aren't. Her children are fascinated by her pursuit of a husband, although they do gripe some about her going out at night. She keeps them up to date on how she is doing. Ten months after arriving in Seattle, she marries.

"I DARE TO LOVE MYSELF AND YOU"

Some people do not want partners, but have been brainwashed into thinking that they should want them. Does that describe you? If it does, don't use your worries about "missing out" or "dying alone" to force yourself into a life plan that doesn't fit you. Living alone can be glorious, lovely, and completely fullfilling. If you like living alone, tell yourself that your way of life is fine for you. You can have friends and lovers and continue to live a single life. Each time you begin worrying about what you ought to be wanting, when you don't want it at all, you might pretend that your worries are little gnats who whisper the worries into your ear. Each time you hear yourself giving yourself the gloomies, reach up, just above your ear, grab the nasty gnat, and imagine squashing it between your thumb and finger. That sounds silly, but it's much less silly than worrying. Besides, it works.

If you do want an intimate, long-term relationship and are not finding one, the first person you need is a very good therapist. This is too important an area of your life to leave to chance. Many lonely people programmed their present loneliness when they were very young and are still stuck with that early decision. They decided, as they watched their parents quarrel, "I'm never going to get married," and never changed that decision. Others said to themselves, "I'll never trust anyone again," when a loved parent disappeared after a divorce. Some, as a result of physical or sexual abuse, considered themselves too bad or too damaged to be wanted by anyone. A therapist can help you clear away any unhealthy personal litter from your past.

When you've done that, your therapeutic goal will be

to get yourself happy and to know that your happiness depends on you alone. Otherwise you are in danger of looking for someone to make you happy, which doesn't work well. You want a partner, not a private nurse, care-taker, or entertainer. You'll want a partner who is also happy, so that you are not burdened with the impossible responsibility of trying to change someone else.

When you are ready to take your show on the road, the next step may be to let yourself look for friends rather than pressuring or worrying yourself about finding a lover. That way you are freer to explore exactly what sort of person you most enjoy. Then, if a special friend be-comes a lover, that's fine. A lover is your best friend, with whom you have established an exclusive, intimate rela-tionship.

To find the right lover takes planning, in spite of what is written in romantic movies and shown on TV. It takes at least as much planning as you put into finding the right job. It also takes shutting up the worrier in your head while you make these plans. Have you been sitting in your apartment waiting and worrying? Sleeping Beauty's prince found her locked in the castle, but nowadays that doesn't happen often. If you are waiting for a lover to find you in your apartment, the only lover you can hope for is a burglar or the guy or gal who delivers the pizza.

Where do you look for a lover? This depends on your interests. Michelle did it well, by starting with lists of all the organizations in town. If you don't want to spend your evenings and weekends going to organizations, there are other choices, including advertising. Make your search a serious, planned campaign.

As you search, do you begin to worry overtime? If so, acknowledge: (a) no lover is perfect and neither am I; and (b) because the future is not predictable, there are no guarantees. The only person in the whole world who assuredly will be with me until the day I die is me. No one else can give me that guarantee. An American poet, Peter Viereck, wrote,

> **Greater than Gods are we**
> **Who dare to love while sentenced to mortality.**

If you are willing to dare to love someone who is imperfect and mortal, you'll need to subdue your worrier. Each time you begin the worry, "Someday my prince (or princess) will go," or "Someday we may not like each other," let yourself decide whether you choose to live in your bleak "someday" or whether you choose to live in the present. Intimacy can only occur in the here and now.

The search for a partner is a wonderful quest. Let yourself enjoy it.

CHAPTER 18

TRUSTING

"I worry little, quick flashes of worry. I pass some stranger downtown and he smiles at me. Immediately I worry, 'What if he's got a gun! What if he's taking it out of his pocket right now and is about to shoot me in the back!' Or I worry that the guy who says he's here to read the meter is really a rapist. All these crazy worries, and I've never really been hurt by anyone."

"Naturally you worry about people. Why, just the other day there was a story in the newspaper about a poor old lady who was conned out of her life savings to get a new roof on her house, and it leaks like a sieve."

"I want a face-lift, but I don't get one because I worry that I may end up looking worse than I do now. I just don't know how to tell ahead if the doctor I pick is going to be competent."

"I worry that there'll be something wrong with the pilot. When I see him in the cockpit, I worry that he looks too old or too young to be reliable, or I decide that he may be tired or hung over."

"I worry that the dentist will pull the wrong tooth."

"I DON'T TRUST PEOPLE"

Although the most common cause of worry is the fear of being "too happy," distrust of others is a close second. This distrust may be the result of early trauma or disappointment. A molestation or an accident can leave a child afraid to trust. A parent may be untrustworthy because of alcoholism or mental illness, and the child decides early, "If I want anything to go right, I have to do it myself, because you can't trust other people." From then on, that child may put the parent's face on the rest of the world.

However, distrust is usually copied. Children learn to distrust because their families are distrustful. Often these grown-ups make their distrust a source of pride, as in the old joke about the man who told his son he would catch him when he jumped off the porch. The son jumped and the father let him fall, saying, "That will teach you not to trust anyone, not even your own father."

> Jean's grandmother always counted her silver after dinner parties, even when the guests were old German families she had known all her life. When Jean asked her if any of her friends had ever stolen the silver, her grandmother was insulted. "Of course not. My friends wouldn't steal. But they might happen to drop a spoon in the garbage." That seemed strange, since the garbage pail was in the kitchen and no guest was ever allowed in there. "Anyway," her grandmother summed up mysteriously, "You can never be too careful about people."

Children are taught, "Don't talk to strangers." This is a sad rule designed to keep them safe from a few unsafe adults by teaching them to distrust all adults. Nonfamily members are identified as the ones who make silver disappear, cheat you if they get a chance, kill you on the operating table, and bungle the job of fixing your car. The primary belief behind such worries is "We are okay and they are not okay." To maintain this stance:

1. Worriers make the standards for others so high that everyone will fail.

If you hire a workman to put up your wallpaper, there will be some airpockets no matter how competently he works.

A computer or a car may not be easy to fix.

An operation cannot be done without some scars remaining. Sometimes an operation cannot make the patient "as good as new."

Any of these deviations from perfection are used by worriers to bolster distrust.

2. Worriers collect examples of nontrustworthy or incompetent actions rather than examples of competency and trustworthiness.

Even the finest physicians cannot keep their patients alive forever, so almost everyone dies while under the care of a physician. The mistrustful worriers keep mental records of the deaths rather than the recoveries.

3. Worriers don't trust anyone to be competent in a field in which they themselves have no expertise.

A worrier who doesn't know how to hammer in a nail without wrecking the wood will worry excessively when he or she needs the services of a carpenter. It's as if the worrier believes, "If I can't do this job, how can anyone else do it?"

Bert knows very little about cars and he doesn't trust auto mechanics. Because of his distrust, he usually doesn't get his car serviced until it has stopped running and must be towed to a garage. He then worries whether it will ever run again. Will they fix the wrong part? Will they fix the right part but in the process destroy something else under the hood, which will only show up after the warranty is over? Will they overcharge him or stuff his car with additional unnecessary and expensive parts? After he has paid for the repairs and is driving his car home from the garage, he plagues himself about unimportant, old creaks, which he thinks the mechanics should have fixed. As the months go by, he complains about the auto mechanics while forgetting to have the oil changed.

He could take an evening class in auto mechanics, but that's not the real solution. To stop distrustful worrying, a class in auto mechanics would be only the beginning. He would also need classes in dentistry, medicine, computer repair, and home carpentry. What he really needs is to stop projecting his own incompetence onto others.

4. Worriers worry instead of getting the facts, even when the facts are readily available.

Jean's daughter, Crystal, is in love with Craig and they have a problem. Craig works in Texas and Crystal works in California. Their incomes go for phone calls and plane tickets, and Crystal's accrued vacation time has already been spent on long weekends in Texas. Now they want a four-week vacation, which will be their first prolonged time together. This hoped-for vacation becomes known to all as The Great Colorado Camping Trip.

Crystal's worry is simple: WHAT IF the director of her department does not approve her taking four weeks without pay, in order to have this "one and only chance at happiness with Craig?" Without the vacation Crystal believes they'll have no opportunity to learn if they really want a life together. As Crystal somewhat histrionically puts it, "If I can't take the vacation, Craig and I might just as well break up today." She tells her worry to family and friends as she plots ways of approaching the director. She plans to bargain with him. She'll offer to work over Christmas holidays. She plans threats, such as resigning if he refuses her these all-important four weeks. Her practical brother, a nonworrier, diagnoses her as batty. Her worrying neice, age seven, sympathizes. Her eleven-year-old nephew yawns and turns up the television. Jean shares as many good ideas as Gloria would have shared if she were there. There are rumors that Craig doesn't understand what the fuss is about.

Finally the date arrives when she can no longer put off asking the director. She goes to his office and, as is so often the case in this family, the meeting is a nonevent compared with the fantastic worry sessions that preceded it. The director tells Crystal that he has heard about The Great Colorado Camping Trip from just about everybody in the department and that he is all for it. Crystal and Craig take their trip, rearrange their lives, and at last report are living happily together.

"I'M LEARNING TO TRUST"

There are several antidotes for distrust. First it is important to recognize the magic involved:

"My suspicions keep me safe."

"If I refuse to recognize someone else's competence, I don't have to notice my own incompetence."

"If I worry enough about strangers, I'll never be taken for a sucker."

"If I never talk to a stranger, I'll never be raped or killed."

"If I postpone asking for vacation time, maybe the problem will solve itself."

What is your magic? See if you can figure it out. Then recognize that neither worry nor magic is protective. All worry really does is increase your own discomfort.

When you are ready to teach yourself to trust, a fun method is to begin by increasing your distrust to the point of absurdity.

1. Since worriers make the standards for others so high that failure is inevitable, make them even higher.

"If there is one streak in this paint job, I'll know that all painters are incompetent. And I won't relax until I find that streak."

"If only you were as perfect as I am, this world would be a heaven."

"The least I expect from a good filling is that it will last forever, so if you tell me a fifteen-year-old filling needs replacement, you must be a crook."

2. Since worriers collect examples of failure instead of success, exaggerate the examples.

"Two airplanes out of two billion have crashed because the pilots weren't paying attention. That is certainly grounds for my suspecting every pilot of incompetence!"

3. Since worriers don't trust others to be competent in a field in which they have no expertise, exaggerate your distrust.

"If I don't know how to add and subtract correctly, how can I expect my accountant to do it right? After all, he's no brighter than I am."

"I'll watch that repair person every second even though I haven't the foggiest notion what she is doing inside the TV. My watching will persuade her to get the wires right."

4. *Since worriers substitute worrying for fact-finding, exaggerate your refusal to get proper information.*

"It would be much too aggressive for me to ask for references before hiring a contractor, so I'll just worry instead."

"It would be too impolite to ask when I'm due for a raise, so I'll worry about it for the next twenty years."

Pick one of your worries based on nontrust and exaggerate it:

"Hey, Pilot, I'll keep watching the wings for you, and I'll rush up to the cockpit to let you know if one of them falls off."

"Even though you've driven twenty years without an accident, I'll help you drive by pointing out the Stop signs. And, by the way, *slow down*. That driver in the car coming our way may be drunk."

"I asked you to be in charge of the alumni invitations, but don't worry, I'll worry for you. And I'll watch everything you do, so you won't make a mistake."

"I am the unofficial Watcher-Worrier for the Universe and I've got my eyes on you."

After you've let yourself have fun exaggerating your mistrust of others, take some time to be serious with yourself. Experience your worried self, frowning, hunched over, tense. Be aware that the tension of distrust is very unpleasant. It is truly painful to live your life distrusting others.

Are you willing to begin to trust by trusting a fantasied person? If so, remember someone from your past who is kind, loving, and worry-free, someone you once trusted. If you don't recall anyone like that, invent such a person. Imagine that person coming close to you and putting a hand on your shoulder. Hear the person say, "Relax. You're trying too hard. You can let others be competent, too." Listen to the caring in this person's voice and let yourself trust your imaginary friend, who tells you, "When you are worried, you fail to distinguish between what is important and what is trivial. For major surgery you want to choose very carefully who cuts into your stomach. But you don't need perfection in the baker who's doing your daughter's birthday cake. All you need is a relaxed happiness when you serve it."

Now be that trusted person yourself and say the words that will convince you. Let yourself believe them. Remind yourself that no one is perfect. "It's okay to trust other people." You may want to play both parts, yourself and the trusted friend, several times, until you can give up automatic distrust of others.

Whenever you hear yourself or others tell horrendous stories designed to prove that people are not to be trusted, find a story about trustworthiness. Jean's favorite: "Once, in Mexico City, a very poorly dressed man chased me for several blocks to give me back my watch, which I hadn't realized had slipped off my wrist." Collect such stories and tell them often.

Be grateful that there are people who can do things you can't do. Be even more grateful that there are people who will do things you don't want to do.

Since worry based on lack of trust is not protective, find better ways to keep you safe.

CHAPTER 19

CARING FOR ME

"I worry about my pimples. If I keep on having pimples, I might as well be dead."

"I worry about nuclear war. In a world like this I can't find a reason to stay alive."

"I worry about my house. I put all my savings into my house and I fixed it exactly the way I want it. Now, just when I thought that for once in my life I had what I wanted, I'm being transferred. It's enough to make a person want to die."

"My son is a diagnosed paranoid schizophrenic. I know that I must have had something to do with his being the way he is. I worry all the time about where he is and what he's doing, and then I worry what would happen to my wife if I decided to commit suicide."

"I worry that my lover will find someone she prefers to me, and if she does, what's the use of living?"

"I MIGHT AS WELL BE DEAD"

Unlike other decision-worry complexes, there are no specific worries that point to depression, suicidal thinking,

or the belief "I might as well be dead." Any old worry
will do. The worry can be preposterous, such as a worry
about AIDs by a nonsexually active and nondrug-using
person. The worry can be minor, such as a worry about
pimples, or major, such as worry about a terminally ill
loved one. The worry may be about the world, about self,
or about others. It is the individual's conclusion to the
worry that is important. Depressed and suicidal people
conclude their worry fantasies with statements such as:
"I might as well be dead." "If my worry comes true, I'll
kill myself." "I'll kill myself and then they'll be sorry."
Some people conclude their worries with Rambo-like
fantasies, and say to themselves, "I'll get the bastards even
if I die in the attempt!" If you worry yourself into depression or make suicidal threats to yourself while you worry,
it's important for you to decide to live.

Another suicidal type of worrier is the one who does
not feel depressed, but who lives dangerously and therefore may die young. Unlike most worriers, who are careful
and caring of themselves and others, these worriers risk
their incomes, jobs, health, and even their lives. If you
have high blood pressure, it is vital that you get your
blood pressure to healthy levels. Eating excessive salt is
about as sensible as eating arsenic. Smokers, heavy drinkers, diabetics who don't follow their diets, and all people
who don't get medical attention immediately on recog-
nizing possibly serious symptoms, are giving themselves
"Die!" messages. Some of these people may worry, but
don't use their worries to take action.

June is fifty-five years old, forty pounds overweight,
and diabetic. Her physician, who specializes in nu-
trition as well as internal medicine, suggests that
she probably could get along without insulin if she
would lose weight and stick to the diet that is right
for her. She needs to eliminate alcohol, tobacco,

white flour, and sugar from her diet, and should cut down drastically on fats and fatty meats. Instead, she has at least two martinis every evening, smokes, and sneaks candy. Her friends, noticing how she eats, say, "She ought to worry!"

That is not true. She doesn't need to worry nor does she need to stop worrying. Neither worrying or not worrying will help her. Her friends, like so many people, confuse worrying with problem solving, when actually they have nothing in common.

Mike brags to his friends, "I like to live on the cutting edge." This means that he likes to juggle his money between banks, to owe far more than he has, and to invest in high-risk ventures. He tells his friends about a famous millionaire who made his fortune in this manner. Mike fails to mention that he himself is not becoming a millionaire; in fact he is rapidly becoming a million-dollar casualty. Mike is a compulsive gambler, and he uses banks and stock brokers the way other gamblers use casinos and gaming tables. Like many compulsive gamblers, Mike is a worried man, but does not use his worries to motivate himself to change. Instead he says, "I'd rather be dead than poor," and "I'll kill myself before I'll change my way of living."

Some people put off needed care by pretending that worry without action is a positive. "Oh, I do worry about it," they say. Or they distract themselves with less important worries. "I'd go to the doctor, but I'm all tied up in knots, worrying about getting ready for my daughter's wedding!" Mike, June, and all of the others who put themselves at risk are just as suicidal as the depressed person who admits to suicidal impulses.

"I LOVE MY LIFE"

The most important way to show your love for yourself is to take care of yourself. Worries don't count. Action does. Make a list of the actions you need to take in order to keep yourself safe and healthy, and then do them. Smoking kills, so stop smoking. Drinking kills, so stop drinking to excess or, if that is impossible for you, stop drinking. Cocaine kills, so stop using it. Get whatever help you need to keep you well.

One way to affirm your right to life is to let yourself have your worries and then conclude them with your decision to take action.

"I do worry, but my daughter's wedding has me tied up in knots." Conclude this with, "My daughter's wedding is not as important as my health. I will take care of my health now."

"Well, I do worry about bankruptcy." Conclude with, "And I'm making an appointment with a financial advisor right now."

The same technique can be used by people who are depressed. If you depress yourself with the worry that this country will be overrun with Communists, conclude your worry with, "And even if our country becomes a Communist dictatorship, I will not kill myself. My life is important to me!"

If you worry yourself into a depression about the way your son is behaving, end each worry with a simple statement to yourself, "My life does not depend on the actions of others. I will live, no matter what my son does!"

If you still hear yourself saying, "I might as well be dead," or "I could kill myself!" change your statement immediately. Say, "No matter what happens, I will not kill myself either accidentally or on purpose." Each time you notice that you are worrying yourself into depression, you need to reaffirm your own right to existence, your own importance to yourself, and your own new decision that you won't kill yourself no matter what the contents of your worries may be. If you are really stubborn, you may keep "raising the worry ante." You may create a worry scene in which you are penniless or imprisoned or have a cancer that has metastasized throughout your body. If you make up this type of worry, learn to laugh at yourself for being so dramatically stubborn. Decide to end your gloom/doom fantasies. "I will decide right now to stop depressing myself. If any real catastrophes do occur in my life, I'll make educated decisions based on the facts at that time."

Most depressed people began their suicidal thinking when they were children. Children don't have options. They can't run away successfully, they can't support themselves, they can't choose new parents, other friends, or a better life-style. And they don't understand the finality of death. A child may decide, "I might as well be dead," "I'll die and then they'll be sorry," or "If things don't get better, I'll jump off the roof." Most children get over these feelings, but some do not.

Whether or not you made these statements, you certainly had sad times. All human beings do. As an exercise to help you today, remember yourself as a sad child. Take a good look at this young child.

Would you kill such a child? Of course, you wouldn't. Imagine telling the child, "I'll never kill you." Say it several times, until it has real meaning for you. Imagine that you are taking that child in your arms tenderly, and say, "I'll never hurt you again by ignoring you or by not getting you medical care or by any other way. I love you and I'll care for you."

To affirm this, take one more trip to the past. This time, find a happy scene in your childhood. Imagine the place you lived when you were between three and six years old. Even if those weren't happy times for you, there are happy moments even in the worst of circumstances. Imagine yourself playing in the mud in the backyard or lying on the bed and looking at apple blossoms outside the window. You may be riding a tricycle or cuddling a doll or zooming a toy car around make-believe roads or playing stoop ball with the other kids. Perhaps you are sprinkling a row of crumbs for the ants or swinging around and around, slowly, in a tire swing.

Close your eyes so that you are not distracted by your present, and let yourself walk back, in your imagination, through time, until you come across a scene in which you, as a child, are laughing and happy. Do not distract yourself with anything you don't like. Find your happy scene. If you don't find it, no problem. Make it up. When you have the scene, fix it in your memory. Notice the child's hair, shape of face, freckles or tan. See the child's small hands. Are the knees knobby or plump, scrubbed or dirty or skinned? Band-Aids on the knees? Let yourself enjoy what you are seeing: one small, unique, happy child.

Now gather both children, the sad one and the happy one, to you. Let yourself experience their merging into your being and acknowledge that both children are still a part of you. They and you deserve a happy life. Tell yourself that you will put your talents into making your life good. This may include getting help with any difficulties that you can't solve alone. And when the bad times come, tell yourself that you have been a survivor up to now and that you will continue to survive for the rest of your natural life.

Will you do that for yourself?

CHAPTER 20

LETTING GO

"I worry all the time when I have to walk alone. Last year I was mugged."

"They say troubles come in threes. My son dropped out of college and now my husband has had a stroke. I worry about what will be next."

"I had terrible pain after surgery, because for me pain medication doesn't work the way it should. I keep worrying that someday I'll need another operation. I couldn't stand it!"

If you've once been struck by lightning, it's difficult to walk calmly in an electrical storm. Worries do follow traumatic events. Though the events belong in the past, in your mind they intrude on your present.

Your trauma may have been a hospitalization, rape, mugging, or accident. You may have been robbed, booked into a jail, or fired without warning by a boss you trusted. A beloved friend or family member may have died. Some of these traumas were physical assaults, which may have left you physically damaged. All of them cause deep emotional pain. Recovery can be slow.

Do your worries indicate that you haven't resolved and put behind you a past trauma? Perhaps you need more time. However, some people spend a lifetime investing their energy in the past instead of the present.

One way they do that is to remain stuck in the "if only" morass that follows any trauma. The theme is, "If only someone had done something differently, the trauma could have been prevented." "If only he'd gone to the doctor earlier..." "If only I'd never gone out with that man in the first place..." "If only we'd had a smoke alarm..."

"If only" is a pretense that you have a second chance. By figuring out exactly how to do it right this time, the magic is that you can go back there and do it over. All "if only's" are irrelevant because the past can't be changed.

Many rape victims do this to themselves. After hearing of others who successfully fought off their assailants, outran them, or pleaded successfully to be left alone, they rehearse what they think they should have done and end up feeling as if in some way they are guilty for having been raped. They ignore the fact that all rapists are different and no method of fighting back or giving in can be guaranteed to be helpful. What works in one situation may cause the person's death in another. Most important, a rape victim cannot be unraped by the magic of "if only."

Maybe you are guilty of having caused your trauma. You drove too fast or you went into a strange bar and did start the quarrel. You can acknowledge that the tragedy was preventable, you can change your behavior in the future, but you can't change what happened. All the guilt and all the "If only's" only serve to keep you from moving forward in life, and they don't have any effect upon the past.

Ready to give up your "If only" thoughts? Each time you fantasize a way that your particular trauma could have been avoided, remind yourself, "It happened and I can't change that fact."

Another way people stop themselves from recovering from a trauma is to try to get over it too quickly. When you have stopped wishing it had never happened, you need time to accept the fact that it did. This means not discounting the event or your reaction to it. Don't try to shove your trauma too quickly into a back drawer of your mind.

You may tell yourself, "Don't make a big deal out of it" or "Other people had worse things happen." If you tell yourself this, answer back, "So what!"

Millions of people have had tonsillectomies.

"So what!" That has nothing to do with the fact that you, on waking in pain and nausea, thought you were choking to death and still worry about choking.

"Millions of people have survived intensive care units."

"So what!" The fact that other people get along just fine in intensive care has nothing to do with your suffering and your belief that you were treated inhumanly and almost died.

"You're lucky that you survived the rape and didn't even get bruised."

"So what!" A rape without bruises does not make it less of a rape.

"Other people don't make a fuss about the terrible things that happen to them."

"So what!" You have a right to feel what you feel.

These traumas don't "go away" just because they are over and you are now safe. They leave you scarred in lots of ways. One of the most common scars is worry. As you worry about recurrences, you give yourself new "what if's" about the future. It is as if your time sense is out of whack. You haven't let go of the past and you are putting mental energy into a fearful future. This keeps you from truly living today.

There are several ways of letting go of yesterday, so that you can also keep from frightening yourself about tomorrow. The easiest is to tell yourself what happened, as simply as possible. Then say to yourself, "I hear you." "It was terrible." "I'm sorry you had to suffer." If that is difficult for you, imagine that the trauma happened to a dear friend. This friend comes to your home and tells you what happened. You would listen to your friend and sympathize. "How terrible for you." "I hear you." "I'm so sorry that happened to you." Make up your own loving, caring words, and then, when you have finished, say those same words to yourself. Tell yourself what happened as many times as seems right for you. You may want to tell yourself only a few times, or you may go over it a hundred times. So long as you keep the recital simple and give yourself only loving responses, you are healing yourself in the process of talking about your trauma.

As you comfort yourself, let yourself feel. Whether you see yourself as brave or as just a normal human being, you have a right to feel what you feel, to acknowledge to yourself that your experience was awful for you, and to be gentle with yourself as you help yourself to recover emotionally. Traumatic events are especially difficult for the stoics, whose self-worth depends on their ability to keep from showing fear, sadness, or pain. So let yourself express your feelings. If you have not cried tears for yourself, do. If you have blocked your anger, pound a pillow and yell your fury. This is a necessary part of coming to terms with what happened.

You also need help from others. Support groups are very valuable. It is easier to explain what happened to people who have lived through similar traumas. From them you can receive the love and understanding you need. If there is no support group that fits for you, try to find another person who has had a similar experience. Talk to each other.

Pick a friend, relative, pastor, or psychotherapist whom you know is an empathetic listener. An empathetic listener follows these rules: Don't give advice. Don't change the subject. Don't talk about someone else who had the same or worse problem. Give understanding and sympathy.

When you have found this person, explain that all you want is to be heard. You are not going to stay stuck in the remembrance of the past and the worry of the future, but for today you want comfort.

As people say in Alcoholics Anonymous, "A day at a time."

When you have learned to comfort yourself, to accept comfort from others, to unblock your feelings, and to acknowledge that the past cannot be changed, you are ready to say good-bye.

There are several ways of doing this. You can tell the scene one last time to a friend and, as you finish, acknowledge that you are saying good-bye to the trauma. You can also use fantasized scenes in your good-byes.

If your trauma is the death of a loved one, fantasize talking to the person before death. You may choose to express your resentments, if you have any, as well as your appreciations. Fantasize thanking the person for enriching your life and tell what you will carry with you in your memory. Then imagine the funeral and afterward watch the casket being lowered into the ground or the ashes being scattered. Say aloud, "You are dead. I will not be with you again in this life. Good-bye."

If your trauma is divorce, pick a scene, tell the person in fantasy your resentments, appreciations, how you have grown as a result of the relationship, and how you will keep growing without it. Then say aloud, "We are no longer partners. Good-bye to our partnership."

If your trauma includes a physical loss, such as loss of sight in one eye, loss of the ability to balance well, or the loss of a leg or arm or breast, you also need to say good-bye. See your body as it was before your accident or surgery, recognize aloud your loss, and say good-bye to the part of you that is now gone or not functioning. "Hey, there, ear, I took you for granted, and that was great. You're now a deaf old ear. The doctors have done what they can to make you hear again and now I have to give up wishing and hoping and lamenting. I'm saying good-bye to you as a hearing ear. I'm glad you are still there for symmetry, and that's about it. I'll put my energy into what I have, not into what I haven't."

For other traumas you may prefer to think of them as a movie you are showing for the last time on your VCR. After this final showing, the movie will be scrapped. You are in charge, and you have a special set. You can speed up the action, slow it down, repeat parts, freeze any frame, or instantly add more to it. Ideally this should be done with a friend or therapist, but you can do it alone. Remind yourself that you are saying good-bye to your trauma. That is the only purpose of watching this movie. You are going to comfort yourself and say good-bye, and you will allow no harassment or self-torture. You can stop your fantasy as soon as it is not helpful to you.

Start the action. As you watch, stop the action whenever you want to say a final word to someone in the movie. "Dr. Smith, thank you for helping me. Your kindness made it easier."

Stop the mugging movie and tell the bastard off. Then say to yourself, "Good job. You survived well." Acknowledge that this movie is terrifying. "I am burning this film. I won't terrify myself with replays." Imagine burning the film.

Tell the rapist that you are no longer going to criticize your role in this movie. And tell yourself, "Hey, hero, you survived and I'm glad. That's all that is important now. There is nothing more to be learned from this movie." Imagine throwing it in the fire.

The next time you worry that lightning will strike again, tell yourself, "That movie is ended."

CHAPTER 21

LIVING NOW

Jean's father, Les, greatly admired two men. One was Charles Lindbergh and the other was the best man at his wedding, Wayne Morse, who became a senator from Washington. When these two men were dying, Les told Jean, "They are doing it right. They're dying and they know it, and each of them is doing what he likes best. Lindbergh is hiding from everybody on an island in the Pacific. And good old Wayne is running again for the U.S. Senate."

Eventually bad things do happen to all people. When you know that tomorrow will be worse than today, it is hard not to worry. The problem with these worries is that they keep you living in your imagined "worse tomorrow" before it ever comes.

Gloria loved life and hated the facts of aging and dying. When the depression ended and the last of her daughters left home, she blossomed again, just as she had when she was a college student. She and Les took dance lessons and became adept dancers. She enjoyed her bridge group, writer's circle, art club, and literature society. Three nights a week she and Les danced with their various dancing groups. For her it was a fine time of life. She had loads of friends, many of whom were a generation younger than she and Les.

The fact that so many were younger became a basis for one of Gloria's big worries. When Jean's first grandchild was about to be born, Gloria said, "Don't let anyone in this town know! I'm so worried that the men in Starlighters won't want to dance with me if they find out I'm a great-grandmother." Jean promised to keep it a secret, but as soon as the boy was born, Gloria was so excited that she told everyone. The men still asked her to dance, so that worry was for naught.

Her devastating, ever-present worry was that someday she would become incapacitated and end up in a nursing home. During her seventies she rarely mentioned her very real intestinal and joint pains, and she and Les kept right on dancing, except for the one year when Les was recuperating from a stroke. Every week she would write her daughters in her tiny, cramped style. An entire society column of the week's events, very similar to the ones she had written for the newspaper years ago, would arrive jammed onto a single page. If only a few things had occurred, she'd send postcards, written over all the space on back and often around the stamps and address.

The last line of each letter and postcard would reveal her worry: "Hoping the good times last . . ." "Took flowers to the county home . . . spare me that ending." "Poor Mrs. Kettleblom, you remember her daughter Nell in Tri Delt, has lost her mind. . . . I keep my fingers crossed!"

Postcards and letters were easily dealt with, but visits would turn gloomy with the WHAT IF of potential incapacitation. Almost any subject of conversation could suddenly become the springboard to that WHAT IF. It was far worse than any earlier worry, because Gloria found no happy ending. Scrubbing the floors or taking in washing could not keep the nursing homes at bay. "Promise me you won't let me live!" "Promise me you'll never let them put me in a nursing home!" Not knowing what else to do, Jean reminded her of her present health, promised that home care would be hired if needed, even promised to smuggle suicide pills into the nursing home, but no reassurance helped.

On the Saturday before Gloria's eightieth birthday, the autumn dance season began, and Gloria and Les danced all evening. Later Les reported that Gloria had had two cocktails and was particularly merry. The next morning, while reading the Sunday paper, she died.

When grieving friends told Les, "She was so lucky. She didn't have to suffer the incapacitation she always worried about," eighty-three-year-old Les said, "I'm luckier. I'm still alive." Although he was grieving, he meant that quite sincerely. He always accepted the present and didn't worry about the past or future.

Are you facing a calamity that you know can't be avoided? Worrying won't help, but planning might. If your problem is your physical health, find the doctor you will want for the rest of your life right now, while you have health and energy. You can ask that doctor the questions that are important to you and figure out how you want to be treated. If you want to prolong your life, you may insist on early hospitalization and all possible procedures to keep you alive. On the other hand, you may want a physician who will treat you nonaggressively in your own home. You may want a doctor who will overmedicate against pain, even if that decreases your life expectancy. You may decide to hire a therapist now, to have a trusted ally who is not caught up in personal grief, as family members are. There are also support groups for almost every bad thing that can happen. If there is no local support group for you, start one. After planning for the future, you may also say good-byes to what you have already lost.

Lawrence knows that he has multiple sclerosis. He finds a lawyer and an accountant to help him with financial planning. He sells his home and buys a new one that will be more practical as his incapacitation increases. He finds a medical specialist he really likes. When he has done everything he can about his future, he still feels quite depressed. In therapy he realizes that he is fighting hard to deny the reality of his present limitations. He overdoes and then is furious at himself for failing. He needs to accept himself and love himself the way he is.

To do that, he decides to say some good-byes, not to others but to the self he had been. He visualizes himself at age fourteen, the day he won his first medal for the hundred-yard dash. He fantasizes rerunning that high school event, experiencing the sound of the starting gun, the feel of the gravel under his racing shoes, the intensity of the sprint, the snap of the tape against his chest, and the wild, silent joy at being first. Then as himself today, the man with multiple sclerosis, he approaches the young athlete. He imagines himself hugging and praising the boy who won the race. He says, "Sorry, kid. We won't be racing anymore." He gives the boy a final hug, draws him close, and experiences the two of them becoming one again. He acknowledges, "Damn, I'm angry and I'm sad."

Next he sees himself as he was five years ago, playing tennis and hiking in the mountains. Again he says good-bye. He lets go of his body image of

"Lawrence, the athlete." It is a painful session for him, which he handles courageously. He doesn't try to stop his tears as he accepts the truth about his present self. When he is finished, he experiences a lightness and a sense of peace.

Lawrence keeps busy. He spends the rest of his life in his new home, growing plants and taking them or sending them to people who are house-bound. Sometimes he's happy and sometimes he's sad. When he can no longer take an active part in his plant-growing avocation, he still enjoys looking at his plants. He keeps weekly appointments with his therapist for the rest of his life and works and plays to make the time meaningful to him.

If your problem is money or jobs, you also may need advisors and allies, plus your own good thinking rather than bad worrying.

Peg loses her job after a very unexpected company merger. With minimal retirement savings and no prospect for an equally remunerative job, she is forced to sell her home at a loss and settle for a very different life-style from the one she has pre-viously enjoyed. For her, the most painful good-bye is to her home. She decides against a last visit, because it is already occupied by the new owners. She visits it in fantasy, walks through the rooms, seeing them as they had been when the house was hers, says her good-byes, grieves, and then imagines throwing away the house key. After this good-bye, she feels more capable of planning for her future and living in her present.

In day-to-day living, staying in the present can be done through activities, being with friends, and even using an "awareness continuum" exercise to keep yourself from worrying. This means, simply, concentrating on whatever you experience through your senses.

> "I am aware of a squeak of a bird, the buzz of a plane. My fingers are aware of the soft wool of my trousers. I am aware of my butt pressing against the chair. I see a white cloud. I am aware of my tears drying on my face. I'm aware of the air in my lungs. I am aware of my smile."

At first this will feel mechanistic, but you'll soon learn to enjoy a few minutes of respite from your problems as you let your senses move freely between your internal and external awarenesses.

If you are facing personal tragedy, how can you live now in the way that is best for you? You may decide to hide from the public on a lovely beach, as Lindbergh did, or continue to work as long as you are able. Making choices is an active way of taking charge of the rest of your life and is far more pleasant than worrying.

Perhaps, as you read this, you recognize that your particular worry about the future is merely a tiny calamity. Don't scold yourself for worrying about things such as a visit to the dentist or the fact that you have to move into a college dorm where you don't know a soul. Everyone worries once in a while, when the going gets rough or when faced with unpleasant choices.

> When Jean's son was ten years old, the doctor told him that the lump on his foot was a planter's wart. "It will have to be removed." "How will you do that?" he asked. "Well, we can burn it off or cut it out." The boy put his foot back in his shoe and tied double knots in the laces. "Find a third way," he told the doctor.

When there is no third way, you may worry. The worrying is about as helpful as hitting your thumb with a hammer in order not to feel your headache. The magic behind such worries is, "If I worry enough, there will be a third, painless wart-removal technique." Or maybe the wart will melt away by itself. Or if you make the worry sufficiently awful, burning or cutting won't seem so bad.

If you find yourself worrying about the warts of life, use part III of this book to learn a few painless worry-removal techniques.

PART III

CHAPTER 22

USING FANTASIES TO STOP WORRYING

There are lots of different ways to banish worries. Almost all of them will be more exciting if you are able to fantasize freely. One of the greatest gifts we possess is the power of positive imagining. In this chapter you can learn how to expand and enrich this ability.

People differ in their ability to imagine. When Beethoven was deaf, he was able to continue to create symphonies because he had the capacity to hear music in his imagination. Many people hear simple tunes, while others never hear music at all. Some people, who don't imagine music, will listen to a symphony on the radio and imagine they can see the conductor, the full orchestra, and all of the audience dressed in beautiful gowns or tuxedos. Others imagine the music but never see the musicians.

Some people imagine in technicolor, some in black and white, and some people haven't learned how to see anything that is not really there. They may tell themselves stories without actually seeing them, so that their imagination is similar to seeing words on a page or hearing a voice read a story. Some imagine without sight or sounds.

Some people can smell chicken frying any time they

choose or remember the exact salty-ropey-fishy odor of the
Boston harbor fifty years ago, and others don't imagine
smells. In their imaginations some people taste chocolate,
feel a kiss on their lips, or experience sinking into the lovely
warmth of a bubble bath, and others don't.

Perhaps you imagine your worries in technicolor, with
sound and light and smells and touch, but probably you
imagine your worries in the form of simple stories that you
tell yourself without bothering to put them on stage. And
that's just fine. As long as you are making up dreary old
worries, you may as well keep your imagination's picture
tube turned off. Keep the sound muted, too, because who
wants worries played out stereophonically? Worries don't
deserve the full, rich treatment that you can learn to give
your happy imaginings.

In banishing your worries, your imagination is one of
your most potent tools, so it's important to learn to use it
well. After you've become an ex-worrier, you can continue
to enjoy imagining for the rest of your life.

Here are some exercises to help you develop the ability
to imagine richly through all your senses. You'll need to
read a sentence or two and then close your eyes when you
are imagining. You'll decide how long to spend with each
fantasy. As you read, you may choose to embellish a particular fantasy, if the fantasy intrigues you. Ready to begin now?

Start with the color yellow. Shut your eyes and imagine
yellow. Imagine turning the color yellow into a lemon that
you are holding in your right hand. Feel the coolness of the
lemon in your hand. Let your fingers explore the shape of
the lemon and the texture of the lemon's skin. In your
imagination throw the lemon in the air and catch it with
both hands. Bring it to your nose and sniff the lemon fragrance. When you are ready, stop imagining a lemon. Open
your eyes.

See the color blue. See a blue sky over a blue sea.
Imagine white sails of a sailboat on the sea. Imagine a white

ocean liner and white clouds in the sky. When you are ready, stop imagining the blue sea and white boats and clouds.

Imagine the color red. Imagine a Valentine card with a red heart and white lace around it. Put it into a red envelope and imagine tossing it into the air. Imagine the envelope turning into a cardinal and flying gaily upward until you can no longer see it.

How are you doing? If you are doing well, congratulations. If you have difficulty seeing what isn't there, repeat the exercises or make up some of your own. Start with whatever imaginary sight is easy for you and then embellish it. Congratulate yourself for whatever you can see.

Imagine that you are holding a bright red apple in your left hand. Hold the apple to your lips and let your lips feel the cool hardness of the apple. Imagine the apple's fragrance. Take a bite. Smell and taste the apple and imagine the crunchiness of the apple as you chew it. Hear yourself chewing the apple. Taste the sweetness of the apple juice as you swallow it. Imagine the moist white of the apple where you took the bite and the outer red where you haven't bitten yet. When you are ready, stop imagining an apple.

Would you like to imagine hearing music? Begin with a simple song, "Twinkle, Twinkle, Little Star." Imagine hearing the song in a high, clear child's voice. Now hear it in a deep, booming voice, the way a father or a grandfather would sing it to you. Experiment with hearing the tune played with one finger on the piano and then hear yourself playing it with waxed paper on a comb, as you may have done when you were young. Feel the paper tickle your lips and listen to the sounds you make in your imagination. If you can, add musical instruments one by one until you are imagining a full orchestra playing "Twinkle, Twinkle, Little Star."

If imagining music is difficult, you may prefer to begin by listening to your tape recorder. Play a song you enjoy and then turn off the recorder and let yourself listen to it again in your imagination.

Hear voices. "Lovely day, isn't it." "Sure beats yesterday." Hear a bird chirp and hear the beep of a car horn. As you listen, what do you imagine seeing?

Now imagine that you are lying in a hammock between two giant palm trees. See the blue sky above you and the white sand below. Feel your body as it nestles against the strings of your hammock. Take time to enjoy your body's ability to feel. Imagine a soft breeze touching your skin. Imagine your toes wiggling. Put one hand over the side of the hammock and feel soft, warm, white sand beneath the hammock. Let your hand give a push to the sand and imagine yourself rocking in your hammock. Imagine seeing green palm leaves and blue sky and white sand. Perhaps you have a favorite song you would like to imagine hearing as you lie in your hammock.

Now use your imagination to make up sights that never were. Start with the sky. Imagine the blue sky and then imagine changing it to pink, to lavender, to a wild, red and white polka-dot sky. You can imagine anything you like! Imagine a heap of bananas in the sand beside your hammock and suddenly turn them into little yellow and green rabbits that stand up on their hind legs, bow to you, turn two quick somersaults, and disappear into the air.

Imagine the hammock rising with you slowly and safely, like a magic carpet. Float away from your palm trees and fly on your magic hammock three feet above the white sand. Want to go higher? In your imagination everything is safe. Rise into the air and look down on the tops of the palm trees and see the sand and the sea beneath you. Float wherever you like. Imagine flying over cities or Inca ruins or your hometown. When you are ready, bring your hammock back to the palm trees and then let your palm trees and hammock disappear.

Anytime you give yourself a worry, you can give yourself, instead, a happy imaginary treat like the ones you have just experienced. Imagine music you love or a hammock by the sea or a ride on a magic carpet. The only rule is that you make your fantasies both pleasant and safe.

In the next six chapters you'll be using your powers of imagination in order to become one of the Ex-Worriers of the World.

CHAPTER 23

CREATIVE FICTION, BEYOND MY SKILL, WORTHLESS WONDER, AND ACTION NOW: FIRST DAY

You are about to begin the first session in giving up your worries. You'll learn today to sort your worries into four distinct categories. Then, on the following days, you'll learn special techniques for dealing with each category of worry.

Are you a bit skeptical? You have a right to be. Your worries have been a part of your life a lot longer than this book has been. However, hundreds of people in the United States, Europe, Australia, and Japan have stopped worrying by using these same techniques in workshops for worriers.

To be successful, what you need most of all is flexibility. At times you'll be asked to think, weigh, and judge. At other times you'll put your adult self on hold while you allow yourself to be a marvelously free, intuitive kid.

Worriers are old and constrained, even if they are barely out of diapers. To become a nonworrier means to become young at heart. You'll be asked to do things that may seem silly or patronizing, such as talking to hordes of people who don't exist or, in later chapters, making up silly endings to your worry stories. When you start to doubt, keep in mind the purpose of all this: *to stop worrying forever*.

Ready to start? Today you'll learn to classify three of your worries: a little, piddling worry; a middle-size worry; and a significant worry. A piddling worry is one that, if it comes true, can't bother your life much at all. A middle-size worry, if it comes true, can cause problems for you. A significant worry, if it comes true, involves a serious loss or death. Start with the piddling worry.

PIDDLING WORRY

"I'm in charge of the reception for the new dean and I worry that it will be a fiasco."

"I worry about my neighbor's daughter, who may be getting a divorce." This is not a piddling worry in her life, but it is in yours.

"I worry about giving my opinion about the school budget at the next PTA meeting. What if I say the wrong thing?"

"I worry that it'll rain for my wedding."

"I'm taking a trip, and I worry that I may forget to pack something I need." This is a middle-size worry if your trip is to Antarctica or if you are flying nonstop to a mountaintop in the Himalayas. Otherwise, wherever you go, you can buy what you need.

"I worry that I may get a C in physical chemistry."

"I worry about what to cook for my dinner party Saturday night."

"I worry that my waist is getting fat and flabby."

"I worry that I'll need dentures, like my mother and father."

In your mind's eye scan your list of worries and pick out a piddling worry that you would like to eliminate from your repertoire. Then answer the first three questions.

1. Is there a possibility that my worry will come true?

A reception for a new dean might be a fiasco, a neighbor's daughter might get a divorce, you might say "the wrong thing," and it might rain for your wedding.

On the other hand, if you always get an A in chemistry courses, you know there is no possibility you'll get a C in physical chemistry. If you have taken innumerable trips and have never forgotten anything important, you are not going to forget anything this time.

2. What is the possibility or probability that my worry will come true (on a scale of 1 to 10)?

Number 1 means that there is only the remotest possibility that your worry will come true. Number 10 means that your worry is absolutely certain to come true. The numbers in between represent degrees of certainty.

"If I give my opinion at the PTA meeting, someone will disagree" should rate a 9 or 10, because there is very little point in giving an opinion that everyone agrees with and, besides, at every PTA meeting, there is bound to be someone who will disagree with almost anything. "If I give my opinion, everyone will hate me" should rate a 1, unless you are extraordinarily adept at antagonizing others. If you are, there is no point in giving an opinion since opinions are given in order to influence others.

"Something will go wrong at my dinner party Saturday night" gets any number between 1 and 10, depending on your definitions of *something* and *wrong*. Someone may come early and someone may come late. Someone may wear a red dress that doesn't match the pink dress someone else has chosen. "The casserole will be dry and tasteless" will rate a 1 if you know that you are a good cook who doesn't dry out casseroles. If you are a poor cook who dries out casseroles, your worry rates a 7–10 until you make changes in your way of cooking. Rate your worry.

3. When will my worry most probably come true?

The casserole for the dinner party will be served Saturday evening. The PTA meeting is this week.

Other worries won't come true for years. "I worry that when I get old, I'll need dentures like my mother and father." When? At age sixty? Age seventy? How many years away are the fantasized dentures? In twenty years dentures may well be obsolete, or they may be far superior to real teeth.

Look back over your answers to the first three questions. If your worry won't come true, probably won't come true, or probably won't come true soon, then you needn't answer any further questions about it. Your worry is a Creative Fiction. This means that you have created a worry that is at this time in your life fictitious.

Be proud of your creativity! Remember that any old banal person can worry about real things that really will happen soon, but it takes a special gift to invent a C in your best subject or a travel worry when you get A in traveling. Not everyone has this talent. In the next chapter you'll learn to increase your creativity and have fun with these worries in order to let them go. For now, put your piddling worry away.

If your worry probably will come true within a relatively short time, answer the next question.

4. Is there anything I can do to prevent this worry from coming true?

You can certainly do something about what you cook for your Saturday-night dinner party.

You can't do anything to save your neighbor's daughter's marriage.

You can't make the sun shine on your wedding day.

If there is nothing you can do to prevent your worry from coming true, categorize this worry as Beyond My Skill to solve.

Are you letting yourself be young at heart? Then pretend you have written the name of your worry on a lovely piece of parchment. Above the name of the worry, imagine letters in gold, saying, BEYOND MY SKILL. Decorate the borders of the page, if you like, with whatever signifies to you the way you will feel when you stop yourself from worrying about things that are beyond your skill to change. Perhaps you would like to imagine hearts and flowers or dancing figures. In a later chapter you'll learn techniques for dealing with worries whose solutions are beyond your skill.

5. *What actions can I take to keep my worry from coming true?*

Take out a paper and pen, if you like, and list all the possibilities for action that you think of in two minutes. Don't discount any of your ideas. Your ideas do not need to be perfect solutions, final solutions, or even solutions at all.

You cannot absolutely guarantee that your Saturday-night party will be enjoyed by everyone, since you are not in charge of other people's decisions to enjoy, but there are things you can do. You can hire a cook, use a recipe in today's newspaper, buy a new cookbook, weed your neighbor's garden in exchange for having her cook your meal, or find books and magazines at your local library that contain party suggestions.

If your waist is fat and flabby, you can join an aerobics class, stop eating fatty foods, take up jogging, or buy a bulky sweater.

6. *Do I choose to take action?*

Beside each of your possible actions write "yes" (I choose to do it), "no" (I choose not to do it), or "maybe."

If you have written only "no" or "maybe" beside your ideas, recognize that "maybe" really means "no for now."

"Maybe" is the answer you think you should give when you don't want to say no. Isn't that true? Your conversation with yourself goes something like this:

"Any good, nice, honorable, industrious person would, of course, do . . ."

"Well, I don't want to believe I am a bad, nasty, dishonorable, lazy person, so *maybe* I'll do it someday."

Treat a "maybe" as if it were a "no."

If you have written "no" or "maybe" after all your answers, you know you don't plan to do anything about your worry. That is okay for your piddling worry. Praise yourself for being honest. It is okay to decide not to do anything differently as you prepare for a Saturday-night dinner party, but it is very cruel and unfair to continue to pester yourself with worries when there is no action you are planning to take. Call this worry a Worthless Wonder. Put it aside for now. Later you'll learn specific ways to deal with Worthless Wonders.

7. *These are the actions I am taking.*

When you have decided on specific actions, plan how to make them most effective. Answer for yourself the following questions: When? Where? Why? Who? How? and Other Information.

When?: This is important. A current action is real and a future action, like a worry, is only a fiction.

Where?: Where will you do what you have decided to do?

Why?: One reason you are taking action is to teach yourself to do rather than to worry. That is a fine and sufficient reason. Perhaps you want more reasons? If so, write down as many reasons as you like.

Who?: If you need or want help to accomplish your action, write down who might help you. Aerobic classes may be more fun if you go with a friend. A friend who knows your plans can give you support and encouragement.

How?: How do you plan to reach your goal? Write your plan of action.

Other Information: Write anything that will help you implement your action effectively.

When you have finished, write across the top of your sheet: A*C*T*I*O*N N*O*W and put your adult self on hold. It's time for you to celebrate.

In the Workshops for Worriers, each person reads aloud the answers to Action Now, and the others cheer. You can do better than that in your imagination. Remember how you turned the hammock into a magic carpet and flew around? Get back on the hammock and fly. Fly over the palm trees, skimming the earth until you see below you a flag-draped podium. Land yourself and your hammock on the podium and make your hammock disappear. Imagine yourself the star of this occasion.

All around the podium is an audience of worriers. Imagine them below you, in business suits and jeans and fancy dresses, in saris and sarongs, turbaned, kerchiefed, capped, and wimpled. Imagine poor and rich and kings and peasants, all of them worriers of the world. Some of them are waving their own Action Now pages, and some have found no actions to take. Imagine them cheering you in their individual ways. See them waving, bowing, smiling. Wave and smile back at them and bow slightly, as befits your status as an action-taking winner. Shut your eyes and play with this scene as long as you like. Don't hurry through fantasy scenes, even if they seem childish. In later sessions you'll recognize that they are very important psychological boosts on your road to becoming one of the Ex-Worriers of the World.

You have finished with your piddling worry. Note that the subject matter of your worry doesn't necessarily tell you how to classify your worry. You have to make your own decisions. For example:

"I'm giving a dinner party next Saturday and I worry that something may go wrong": This is a Creative Fiction worry if you and your guests always end up enjoying your parties, in spite of your worries beforehand. It is a Worthless Wonder, if you think of ways to improve your party but don't carry them out. It is an Action Now worry if you use your worry to take action that improves your style of entertaining.

"My neighbor's daughter may be getting a divorce": Beyond My Skill.

"My waist is getting fat and flabby": If this simply isn't true or if the "flabbiness" is so minor that only you can see it, then this worry is Creative Fiction. If you are overweight and flabby, but you decide to do nothing about it, your worry is a Worthless Wonder. If you decide to change your eating habits or get more exercise, classify your worry as Action Now.

"I worry that it'll rain for my wedding": Beyond My Skill.

"I worry that I'll say the wrong thing at the PTA meeting tomorrow": Most likely this is Creative Fiction. If not, it certainly seems to require Action Now.

"I'm taking a trip, and I worry that I may forget to pack something I need": Creative Fiction, Worthless Wonder, or Action Now.

"I may get a C in physical chemistry": Creative Fiction. If there is truth in the worry and you want a higher grade, then Action Now is indicated.

MIDDLE-SIZE WORRY

Which of your middle-size worries will you choose?

"I worry that I'll fail my driving test."

"I worry that I'm not saving enough money."

"My son is moving to California and I worry that I'll be so lonely without my grandchildren."

"I'm always worrying about my family. I worry about my daughter not doing well in school, my son changing jobs so often, my mother being so dependent on me, and I worry about my cousin's illness."

"I worry that my baby will grow up to be a delinquent."

"I worry that my house will burn down."

Pick from your mental list of middle-size worries and answer the following questions:

1. Is there a possibility that my worry will come true?

Yes, there is a possibility that my daughter won't find the right husband. I know my son won't stay with his job. My cousin's illness is a fact, and my mother isn't getting any younger.

2. What is the possibility or probability that it will come true?

The statistical probability of my house burning down is less than a 1.

3. When will my worry most probably come true?

"I worry that my baby will grow up to be a delinquent." This is a worry that can't come true until he is grown. Since he is a baby now, he has at least ten to eighteen years of nondelinquency ahead of him. (Of course, it is also Creative Fiction because, on a scale of 1 to 10, you probably already gave it a 1.)

If your worry won't come true, probably won't, or won't come true for a long time, admit that it is Creative Fiction and remind yourself that you are a most creative, inventive human being. You think up horrible worry stories that will never come true. In the next session you'll learn to use your creativity to banish these worries.

4. Is there anything I can do to prevent this worry from coming true?

You can't change your daughter, son, cousin, or mother, so mark these worries Beyond My Skill. Announce to yourself, "I, knowing I am helpless to solve my family's problems, am turning their worries over to God, fate, and the others in the family."

Do your shoulders feel lighter? It's in the shoulders

that most people feel the weight of the worries they cannot solve. Relax your shoulders and let them be burden-free.

5. *What actions can I take to keep my worry from coming true?*

If you worry about your son going to California, you probably can't do anything about his leaving, but you can choose to take action on your own behalf in order to stop being lonely.

6. *Do I choose to take actions?*

Again, note that "maybe" means "no," at least for the present. Since the consequences are middle-size if this worry comes true, consider carefully your action options to solve this worry, before you put "no" or "maybe" after any of your ideas.

If there are no actions you choose to take to prevent your worry from coming true, your worry is a Worthless Wonder. Don't scold yourself for not taking action. Instead, allow yourself some curiosity about how you'll use this worry when you get to the Worthless Wonder chapter.

7. *These are the actions I am taking.*

Example: What I will do when my son moves to California?

Get baby-sitting jobs. NO

Go to the city college to find out how to enroll in horticulture courses so that I can plan and create my own garden in the backyard. YES

Invite friends for lunch. MAYBE

Brush up on my secretarial skills. MAYBE

Learn to enjoy my leisure time. YES

Become a volunteer at the hospital. NO

ACTION NOW: "I choose to go to college and learn to landscape gardens. I may even have a new profession. It is the most exciting thought I've had in years. I don't have to mope and worry about me. It will give me plenty to do, even though my son and his family are gone, and I'll love every minute of it."

Answer where, why, who, how, and other information that will help you to accomplish your goal. You are going to do something to solve a middle-size problem. Congratulations! Fantasize the multitudes also congratulating you.

You can make your decision even more exciting by bragging to friends and loved ones about the actions you are taking. You might telephone someone as soon as you finish reading this chapter.

SIGNIFICANT WORRY

Now is the time to deal with your significant worry.

"I worry that my husband will fall in love with someone else, even though I know he won't."

"I may end up with cancer."

"I am losing my job."

"I worry about my brother Harold, who drinks too much and acts silly at family parties."

"I worry about my father, who is an addict."

"I worry about war and acid rain and endangered species."

"I worry that the stock market will collapse and I'll lose my savings."

When you have found a significant worry, answer the questions.

1. Is there a possibility that my worry will come true?

Jean's old worry of dying in a forest fire is a significant worry and quite impossible when there are no forests within five hundred miles. Worrying about potential unfaithfulness in a faithful husband or wife is Creative Fiction.

2. What is the possibility or probability that my worry will come true?

"I may die" rates a 10, since it is absolutely true. "I may die tonight in my sleep" rates a 1 if you are healthy and younger than ninety.

3. When will my worry most probably come true?

I am perfectly healthy now and I'm only forty. I will die of something, whether or not it is cancer, but the statistical chances are that I'll live another thirty-five to forty years.

File forest fires, the unfaithful spouse, and a nonexistent cancer under Creative Fiction.

4. Is there anything I can do to prevent this worry from coming true?

Since Harold isn't at all interested in my belief that he occasionally drinks too much and acts too silly, Harold is Beyond My Skill to change.

"I, knowing I am helpless to prevent my brother Harold from drinking too much at family parties and then being too silly, am turning this problem over to Harold. In fact, I am realizing that Harold's drinking at family parties is not a significant worry for me. It may be a middle-size or significant worry for him, but it is not my worry."

5. What actions can I take to keep my worry from coming true?

I can't contribute to the solution of every problem in the universe. In each day's mail there are requests for money for worthy causes. There are the whales, the starving, the bombs, the political campaigns, all the dozens of causes that I know are important. I believe in almost all of them, but I can't afford to give to everything. I'll pick one worry, nuclear war, and take action. The rest of the problems I am putting aside under the title Worthless

Wonders, because it is worthless for me to worry about problems I am deciding not to try to solve.

6. *Do I choose to take action?*

You are considering actions to prevent serious consequences to you or your world. It is important that you weigh these consequences carefully before you decide to disregard them. If you have written a "no" or "maybe" that can damage your health or well-being, do rethink your answer. Don't file "Stop smoking" or "Pay my income tax" under Worthless Wonders. Love yourself enough to take actions that are important for your health and well-being.

Example: My father is an addict.

Share my concern with him. YES

Stop driving with him. YES

Stop giving him money. MAYBE

Join Al-Anon to find out what else I can do. YES

Arrange to get him hospitalized. MAYBE later. I need support to do that.

Example: *I'm losing my job.*

Get an updated résumé. YES

Begin looking for another job. MAYBE

Figure out how to live on my retirement income. YES

Go back to school. NO

---

7. *These are the actions I am taking.*

ACTION NOW: "I will work for a world that is free of the threat of nuclear war."

When?: Tonight I will write my congresswoman and support disarmament.

Why?: Because doing something, even a small action, is a positive. Worrying is a negative.

Who?: Just me. No, I think I'll phone ten friends and invite them to a letter-writing party at my house. I like that idea.

Other Information: I'll find out what the antinuclear organizations are doing and will join one of them.

I'll go to the next meeting of the Beyond War group.

When you have decided what you will do, answer When?, Where?, Why?, Who?, How?, and Other Information so that your actions will be as effective as you can make them. The more significant the worry, the more important it is to take effective action.

Applaud yourself for choosing action about a significant problem. Tell your decision to three friends or relatives who would also applaud you. If possible, tell them tonight. The fact that you will work to keep a significant worry from coming true is so important that it is worth a long-distance call anywhere.

You have now finished this session. Have you enjoyed what you have done? Do not, no matter what the provocation, criticize yourself for anything you have decided to do or not do. That would be an insidious way of attacking your self-esteem and creativity and might lead to more rather than less worrying.

Relax for a few minutes before returning to your everyday world. If you like, give yourself a loving facial massage. Outline your eyebrows gently and trace the bones around your eyes. Let your fingers make soft little circles on your temples and smooth your forehead. Smooth your cheeks very gently. Touch your lips and chin, outlining their shape. Gently massage your ears, exploring the dips and valleys.

Imagine loving hands massaging your neck and shoulders, letting you know that you may relax your muscles. Feel your shoulders soften and drop. Take the time to relax the rest of your body.

In the next session you'll learn how to use Creative Fiction worries for fun, in order to begin to let your worries go.

CHAPTER 24

CREATING NEW FICTION: SECOND DAY

In this session you will learn how to rewrite your Creative Fiction worries in order to make them fun. To be lighthearted about worries, especially those that almost certainly will not come true, is the best possible way to cure a worry addiction. That is the purpose of today's chapter.

If you have more than one Creative Fiction worry, choose whichever one you would most like to obliterate from your mind. If none of the three worries you learned to classify on page 161 is Creative Fiction, look over the following list to see if any of them reminds you of one of your own worries:

"I'm in charge of the reception for the new dean and I worry that it will be a fiasco."

"I'm taking a trip and I worry that I may forget to pack something I need."

"I worry that I may get a C in physical chemistry."

"I worry that my baby will grow up to be a delinquent."

"I worry that my house will burn down."

"I worry that my husband will fall in love with someone else."

Here are others:

"I worry that our bank will fail and we'll lose our savings."

"I worry that I may get AIDS, although I have never had unsafe sexual contacts and I've never shared a hypodermic needle because I don't use drugs."

"I worry that at my last physical examination, the doctor didn't notice that I have some terminal illness. Or he noticed but doesn't want to tell me."

"I worry that I'll be mugged, even though there are no muggings in our town."

"Every time my daughter is late coming home from school, I worry that she's been kidnapped."

"When I see a state highway patrol car behind me, I worry that I'm going to be arrested for something."

Any of those sound familiar? If you have no Creative Fiction worries, you must be a practical person who doesn't make up self-torture tales. You can skip this chapter, or go on reading if you want to find out about the worry-life of much of the human race.

Perhaps some of these worries sound familiar, and you say, "But they aren't really fiction because they do happen to people."

There was a woman in New York who worried about the city taxis. She said the drivers don't drive well and a person can get hurt. Through the years she worried, stewed, and used taxis, and after thirty years of worry, she was riding in a taxi that got hit by a car. The accident was minor, but because she was by then an old lady, she was taken to a hospital to be checked out. The first thing she said to the emergency-room doctor was, "See, I knew I was right to worry about taxis." Even if sometime, somewhere, a Creative Fiction worry does come true, is that a reason to bedevil yourself with it throughout your life?

Creative Fictions are stories you create about unlived times and events that never happened, just like L. Frank Baum did when he wrote the Oz books and Margaret Mitch-

ell did when she wrote *Gone With the Wind*. The difference
is that they wrote their stories for the joy of writing, for
fame, and for profit, and you write yours to make yourself
unhappy. Your stories take you away from the good feelings
you might have and leave you tense or angry or sad or
scared instead of happy. Isn't that an amazing human trait,
this capacity to invent stories and then to suffer from them?

The first step in stopping your Creative Fiction worries
is to remove the suffering from your stories. Logic, truth,
even statistics won't help you much. What will help is for
you to be a bit wacky. Will you give it a try?

You've chosen your worry. The next step is to weave it
into a ridiculous tale. Begin by telling yourself your worry
from start to finish. When you're done, tell it again and
change the ending. It's simple.

For instance, Gloria could repeat her worry about having
no money for Jean to go to college and then change the
ending by having Jean win a scholarship and the newspaper
business become sufficiently profitable to pay for college
for all the daughters. These endings aren't as dramatic as
scrubbing floors and taking in laundry, and they actually came
true, but how was Gloria to know that during her Creative-
Fiction-about-college era?

Gloria could make the ending fantastic, by getting money
through the intercession of leprechauns or helpful mutants
from outer space. She could then tell the story to her great-
grandchildren, who love stories made up by favorite adults.

She could make the problem fun, by imagining that
because there is no money for college, Jean travels around
the world, seeking her fortune, instead of seeking it at the
University of Illinois. In a faraway jungle below the Andes
Jean finds a spectacular sugar that is without calories. She
teaches the poor people to harvest it and they all become
rich, including Jean, and everyone lives on candy while their
teeth stay free of cavities.

She could make the story ludicrously tragic. Jean, because of not having the money for college, walks the streets

in rags, holding her starving baby and begging crusts of
bread from steel-hearted passersby.

Here are more examples:

THE DEAN'S RECEPTION WAS A FIASCO

Heaven knows there was nothing wrong with the
tea. There was also nothing wrong with the properly paper-thin pieces of fruitcake nor was anything wrong with the beautifully polished silver
dishes holding lovely little mints on newly ironed
lace doilies. The problem was an unpedigreed
cat who happened into the reception at the same
moment when a small gray mouse was walking
unobtrusively along the far wall.

Almost everyone politely looked the other
way and tried to make the best of it. But poor
Miss Willowby, who suffers from a slight arthritic
condition of the neck, could not turn quickly
enough. She saw the cat pounce and promptly
screamed, then keeled over onto the potted
palm, which, because it was made of paper,
keeled over too.

The mouse ran diagonally across the room
and somehow landed on Professor Chigley's lap.
The cat followed, and the reception became a
fiasco to all but that dreadful Professor Barring-
ton, who laughed loudly.

THE HOUSE IS BURNING

I'm on the second floor and the flames are shoot-
ing around me as I throw the baby books, the

photo albums, and all the family silver out the window into the firemen's net.

"Jump," they yell. "Stop being a hero and save yourself!"

"Not before I've rescued Grandpa's portrait," I answer courageously.

I race to the attic, find the old picture, and run back to the window. By now the entire house is in flames. Carefully I toss the portrait to the waiting men and jump, landing squarely in the net on Grandpa's face.

It wasn't a flattering likeness anyway.

The firemen are amazed by my coolness under fire, although I am a bit singed.

I smile secretly. I think of the new house the insurance money can buy.

THE SEDUCTION OF A HUSBAND

That fantastic little rock starlet comes tapping on his door. She looks at him provocatively and wiggles seductively, and he says to her, "Begone!" He turns to me and winks, and we move on to the bedroom and close the door.

MY BABY SON AND DELINQUENCY

My son grows up to be a delinquent.
    Hey, that's no fun. I'll change it to:

HOW MY BABY SON GREW UP TO SAVE HIS MOTHER FROM A LIFE OF CRIME

There I am, a perfect gun moll, with tight skirt, tighter blouse, lots of makeup, and a huge glass of bourbon straight. In the waistband of my tight skirt is a loaded handgun. "Stick 'em up and give me your money," I snarl to the cashier, who blushes furiously because she doesn't know how to give me the money while her hands are up.

And at that moment who should stride manfully into the bank but my baby boy. "Mother, dear Mother," he pleads, "come home with me now."

Of course this is all ridiculous. That's the point.

If you turn off the critic in your head and turn on your spoofer, you can have fun with any Creative Fiction worry.

Now it is your turn. Take your Creative Fiction worry and turn it into a story that will make you laugh. You may choose to tell yourself your story, as if reading it from a book. You may lie back and imagine watching it, as if it were being acted on a television screen. You may even write it down and illustrate it.

If making up a story seems difficult rather than fun, imagine instead that you are holding a small book with your worry on the cover. As you look inside, you see cartoons or drawings that illustrate and spoof your worry.

TRAVEL WOES

Imagine two cartoons:

> **A tourist is bent nearly double, trying to carry two monstrous suitcases. Underneath is the caption: "I didn't forget a thing."**

> **A hotel room is totally littered with clothing and other articles that the tourist has thrown all over the room. Underneath is the caption: "I know I packed my toothbrush somewhere!"**

You can also make your worry into a very boring book. Imagine that you are holding in your lap a book entitled *A to C In Physics and Other Subjects*. Turn the pages and see that they are all alike. Each page begins with the words, "What if I should fail . . . ?" and then goes on to describe test after test after test, from second grade to graduate school. As you hold the book, imagine that you are sitting beside a beautiful fireplace. The fire is burning and you are watching the flames. Although you have never in your life been a book burner, now is the time. You realize that this book is without any redeeming value. It has caused you years of pain. You don't want anyone else to suffer from it. Toss it into the flames and watch as it burns to ashes.

Another way of handling Creative Fiction is to sing it. Sing your worry to the tune of your favorite blues song or country-western. If you are ambitious, turn your worry into an opera. Most worries are quite wonderful when sung to the tune of the "Toreador Song."

For the rest of the week, whenever you recognize that you are worrying about something that probably will not happen or will not happen soon, create a new ending, visualize a cartoon, burn the book, or sing away your worry. Don't make fun of yourself, but do make fun of your worry. That is one of the quickest and most pleasant ways to stop worrying.

In the next chapter you'll learn quite different techniques for dealing with the worries you have categorized as Beyond My Skill.

CHAPTER 25

BEYOND MY SKILL: THIRD DAY

Worries that are beyond your skill to solve:

"It may rain on my wedding day."

"My daughter is not doing well in school, my son is changing jobs too often, my cousin is ill, and my mother depends too much on me."

"My brother Harold drinks and acts silly at family parties."

"The stock market may collapse."

"All sorts of things are going wrong in the world."

Wouldn't it be wonderful to be God? You could do so much! You could announce from the clouds, "Any human being who kills another human being deliberately will automatically die and the murdered one will be brought back to life instantaneously. The tortured will feel no pain and only the torturer will suffer." Bingo, war and cruelty would come to an end. If you were God, you could make the rain come with the spring planting and never with the fall harvest. You could decree a special Wedding Day, when the weather would always be perfect.

From the clouds you could demand, "Brother Harold, put down that bottle and don't ever pick up another!" and, lo and behold, Harold would live out a sober life.

You could arrange for your daughter to do well in school, your mother to quit depending on you, your son to quit changing jobs, and your cousin to be well. Then, when you've arranged the weather and your family perfectly, and abolished war and suffering, you could give up your worries about everything that is beyond your control.

Just for fun, imagine that you are the absolute monarch of absolutely everything. You can make everyone in the world do what you know is best for them. Even though that is egotistical, grandiose, and, unfortunately, unreal, play with the idea. Now that you know how to imagine freely and in technicolor, dress yourself royally, create a throne, and give yourself lots of attendants, who scurry hither and thither to do your bidding.

Your daughter is having school problems. As absolute monarch of absolutely everything, you can abolish television for six weeks or forever, you can pay teachers more than doctors so that only the best of the best are helping her. You can put mental-health money into devising IQ pills. You can make General Motors hire her as a junior executive and then send her off to a special motivational learning program, which you insist they devise. As monarch, you can certainly overawe your daughter, so that she wouldn't even think of not studying.

You want your mother to find friends and not depend on you for everything? You can order the installation of moving sidewalks with seats on them for the handicapped, so that your mother won't need you to drive her anywhere. You can give her mood-elevating sweet potatoes, movie stars for companions, or a trip on a spaceship that is making a ten-year journey around the planet Mars.

You don't want rain on your Wedding Day, but the drought is ruining your garden. You can float icebergs to the nearest port and build a canal from there to where you live.

Play with being absolute monarch of absolutely everything and think up the wildest solutions possible. Keep with it until you find the subject boring. If you prefer reality to fantasy, you may be bored quite soon. On the other hand, isn't it more fun to pretend to solve the unsolvable than it is to worry about what you cannot solve?

Take out your Beyond My Skill worry. If none of the three worries you learned to classify on page 161 fits that category, perhaps you've thought of another you'd like to use.

Many Beyond My Skill worries come from the wish to change other people. Does that fit your worry? If so, here are four truths that can set you free:

1. I am not in charge of anyone else's feelings.

You can't make people feel, even though you might have learned the opposite as a child, if your parents told you, "You make me sad" or "You make me angry." It is not true. You may have been the world's worst pest at times, but you could not make them feel. They chose their own feelings. If you broke a glass, your mother may have been sad, as she told herself, "We don't have the money to replace it." Your father may have been angry, as he told himself, "Children should be more careful!" Your little brother may have been frightened, as he told himself, "There's going to be a fight and I may get hurt, too." Your grandmother may have been amused, remembering a funny incident that occurred long ago when your father broke a glass. Your actions may set the stage for others to experience emotion, but you cannot choose their feelings. They make themselves sad, angry, frightened, or amused.

2. I am not in charge of anyone else's thoughts.

You can't make people think as you want them to think. People are in charge of their own thinking. You can plead, argue, and present the world's best logic, and you still won't be in charge of their thinking.

3. I am not in charge of anyone else's behavior.

You have some control over what your children do, but the older they get, the less control you have. As the saying goes, "Children learn to walk to walk away." You cannot control the behavior of others.

4. *Since I am not in charge of other people's emotions, thoughts, or actions, my worries cannot make them change.*

In your imagination bring a person you worry about into the room. Place an empty chair in front of you and imagine that person sitting there. Perhaps the person is your son. For the last time, tell him your worry.

"Every time you change jobs, I worry that someday you'll be unemployed. I worry that you will run out of employers and then you'll run out of money. And I worry that everyone will blame me, because I am your parent."

When you have completed the recital of your worry, add, "I want you to change."

Move to the second chair, the one you placed in front of you, and pretend you are your son. As your son, say just one sentence, "I want you to change, too." That is undoubtedly true, because at the very least he wants you to stop worrying about him.

Go back to your own chair. "I won't stop worrying until you change."

Go to the other chair, be him, and say, "You change!"

Move again to your chair, and say, "Change!"

Be him and say, "Change!"

Go back to your chair. Do you realize how stuck you are? You might as well give up. Are you willing? If you still think your worry will make him change, continue your part of the dialogue. "If you don't change, I'm going to keep worrying for the rest of my life."

Look at your son and imagine that fifteen years have gone by, then twenty years, thirty years. Are you really going to condemn yourself to a lifetime of worry? If not, how about quitting right now? Tell your son, "I've decided to stop worrying about people I can't change. I am turning my worry over to you and you can worry or not, as you please."

Anytime you are caught up in worries about a person whom you wish would change, use this exercise and then drop your worry.

A second group of Beyond My Skill worries are based

on natural phenomena that you want changed. Bring in your worry in a clear plastic bubble and put it on the chair in front of you.

Perhaps in the bubble on the chair is your worry about rain on your wedding day. Inside the bubble see the place where you'll be married. Above it, see storm clouds.

You can do almost the same double-chair with the bubble as you did with your son, except that you don't have to pretend that the bubble talks back. Say, "I want you to change, Weather." "I am going to worry all day every day so that magically I can persuade you, Sun, to shine for me." "If you knew how much I worry, you would certainly shine."

Perhaps you worry about politics or world problems. Put the White House in your bubble. Say to the White House "I will worry until someone of my choice occupies you."

Put a world problem in the bubble. Perhaps in your bubble are tiny, unhappy people in South Africa, Central America, Ireland, or Israel.

Say to the tiny figures in your bubble, "I will worry until all your problems are solved." How about, "If there is an afterlife and I can look down on this earth, I will continue to worry until your struggles have ceased and everyone in your land is happy. I will spend all my time in heaven unhappy and worrying." Now are you ready to give back your worry, so that you don't lug it around through all eternity?

Whenever you feel stuck with a worry that is beyond your ability to change, you can do a double-chair exercise to get in touch with the uselessness of your worry. There are two precautions:

• **Keep your imagined conversations short. Never say more than one or two sentences from each chair. Stop after three minutes, whether or not you have succeeded in giving up your worry.**

Otherwise, you may begin making speeches in an attempt to make others change. That could increase rather than decrease your worrying.
• Don't pretend that the other person or the scene in the bubble makes the changes you've been wanting. To give up your worry, you have to do the changing.

Think of your Beyond My Skill worries as a heavy load that you have agreed to carry and are now ready to put down. Imagine that you've been carrying it on your back and that you are tired of the weight. What is your weight like? Perhaps it is an old gunnysack filled with woe. Perhaps it is a papier-mâché replica of the globe strapped to your back. Or is it an old suitcase filled with oil portraits and daguerreotypes of all the people you worry about? Whatever shape you give it, imagine its heaviness on your shoulders and back, tiring you and keeping you from feeling free.

Reach behind your head, grab the weight, and pull it off your shoulders. Put it on the floor in front of you. Tell it "Carrying you around is stupid. You don't help me and you don't help the ones I've worried about. I'm done with you."

When you are ready, make it disappear. You can melt it down into nothing or hire imaginary trash collectors to carry it off. You can put it inside a galactic spaceship and watch your worry become a silver streak in the heavens as it moves into outer space.

When you are done with your worry about someone or something you cannot change or control, remember:

1. I am in charge of my own feelings.
2. I am in charge of my own thoughts.

3. I am in charge of my own actions.
4. Since I am in charge of myself, I can stop worrying.

Remind yourself of a few of the myriad things you have changed about yourself during your lifetime. Appreciate the skills you have and the uses you make of those skills. As you give up worrying about the things that are beyond your control, you are changing yourself. Also, you are freeing your energy for projects and interests in which you can be effective.

The next time you find yourself caught up in worries that are beyond your skill, switch to the role of absolute monarch of absolutely everything and have some fun, and then do a double-chair exercise if you like.

When you are ready, take your worries off your shoulders and let them go.

Next you will tackle the worries you classified as Worthless Wonders.

CHAPTER 26

WORTHLESS WONDERS AND THE OLD KIT BAG: FOURTH DAY

In this session you will learn how to take control of your Worthless Wonders. Here are some typical ones:

"I worry about what to cook for my dinner party."

"I worry about not saving enough money."

"I worry because my waist is getting fat and flabby."

"I worry that no one likes me, because I'm always late."

"I worry that I'll never amount to anything, because I don't study enough."

"I worry that I'll never find a lover, because I don't go out like I should."

"I worry about the SPCA. I ought to do more for them."

"I worry that I'll end up with dentures, because
I don't floss my teeth."

All of these Worthless Wonders may be legitimate
concerns. You should learn to cook well, save your
money, floss your teeth, do aerobics, be on time, date more,
find a better career, and give more money to charities,
shouldn't you? They are *wonders* because, if only you did
what you should, you would be a wonder. You would
be a fine, healthy, giving, happy person; in fact, you
would be as nearly perfect as human beings get. But
you don't do what your worries tell you to do, so the
worries are *worthless*. You may believe that if you hound
yourself enough and make the worry sufficiently horrible, someday you will do whatever it is you should
do, but so far, in spite of your weeks and months and
even years of worrying, all you've achieved are worry
headaches. The worries have turned out to be worthless
for you.

Besides taking away your happiness and giving you
headaches, these worries are also boring. How exciting
can it be to worry for the hundredth time about what will
happen to you if you leave the plaque on your teeth or
the fat on your hips?

By now you understand that you create your own
worries and are in charge of what you worry about. Understanding is all well and good, but probably you still
feel as if you are not in charge. It's almost as if these
worries, like nasty little bugs, creep up when you're not
looking and defy your best efforts to eradicate them.

Now is the time for tackling these dreary worries. Get
comfortable and take out one of your worthless wonders.
If none of the three worries you learned to classify on
page 161 was a Worthless Wonder, perhaps you have
found one that would qualify.

There are a few new questions to ask yourself about
your worry:

A. How long have I had this worry?
B. In the past week, how often have I worried about it?
C. Has this worry been helpful, harmful, or neither?

Here are three examples, including the answers to the questions in chapter 23.

"I WORRY WHAT TO COOK FOR MY DINNER PARTY"

1. *Is there a possibility that my worry will come true?* Yes, my entrée may not be as tasty as I want it to be.
2. *What is the possibility or probability that my worry will come true?* Perhaps a 4.
3. *When will my worry most probably come true.* Saturday evening.
4. *Is there anything I can do to prevent this worry from coming true?* Yes.
5. *What actions can I take to keep my worry from coming true?* Hire a cook, use a new recipe, exchange weeding for cooking, get suggestions at the library.
6. *Do I choose to take action?* Not really. Cooks are expensive, and I hate using new recipes.
A. *How long have I had this worry?* I've worried every time I entertain, for the past fifteen years.
B. *In the past week, how often have I worried about it?* Twenty times at least.
C. *Has this worry been helpful, harmful, or neither?* The worry has been helpful, because my

worry makes me work hard at cooking well.
Would I do the same if I didn't worry? My worry
is harmful because it drives my husband crazy
and keeps me from enjoying entertaining.

"I WORRY ABOUT NOT SAVING ENOUGH MONEY"

1. *Is there a possibility that my worry will come true?* Yes, I may end up without a big enough savings account.
2. *What is the possibility or probability, that my worry will come true?* An 8 or 9, because I never have enough.
3. *When will my worry most probably come true?* Now and forever into the future.
4. *Is there anything I can do to prevent this worry from coming true?* Yes.
5. *What actions can I take to keep my worry from coming true?* See a financial counselor, stick to a budget, buy no new clothes for a year, etc., etc., etc.
6. *Do I choose to take action?* Not really.
A. *How long have I had this worry?* Ever since I got out of college.
B. *In the past week, how often have I worried about it?* Four or five times.
C. *Has this worry been helpful, harmful, or neither?* Worrying spoils my enjoyment of whatever I buy.

"I WORRY BECAUSE MY WAIST IS GETTING FAT AND FLABBY"

Sometimes people who worry about their weight are willing to take action and sometimes they are not. If you worry and don't diet or exercise, answer the first six questions and the additional ones.

1. *Is there a possibility that my worry will come true?* Yes, my worry may come true. I may not lose weight. Sometime in the future my health may be at risk from overweight.
2. *What is the possibility or probability that my worry will come true?* Chances are about a 5 that I won't lose weight and about an 8 that, if I do lose weight, I'll regain it immediately.
3. *When will my worry most probably come true?* Already, part of it has come true. I am overweight. In the future I might have health problems.
4. *Is there anything I can do to prevent this worry from coming true?* Yes, of course.
5. *What actions can I take to keep my worry from coming true?* I can diet or exercise.
6. *Do I choose to take action?* I don't ever stay on diets and I know I won't exercise more.
A. *How long have I had this worry?* Since age twelve. I must have worried about my weight at least a million times since then.
B. *In the past week, how often have I worried about it?* Today: one time. Yesterday: maybe three times. This week: twenty times total.
C. *Has this worry been helpful, harmful, or neither?* I diet from time to time. I gain and lose and gain and lose. If I didn't worry, would I diet?

There is a similarity in the responses of all three worriers. They have been pestering themselves about their worries for a long time and they haven't used their worries as a stimulus to solve their problems. This is typical of people whose primary worries can be categorized as Worthless Wonders. Because they are chronic worriers, they need special methods for curing themselves of their addiction.

Before they try to stop worrying, they need to be in charge of their own worrying. In order to do this successfully, there are two more questions, which are very important. Put them under the heading:

NEW WORRY SCHEDULE

1. *What times of the day will I worry?* (Be exact.)
2. *How many minutes will I worry at each worry session?*

You may think that these questions are frivolous or even insulting. They are not. Your decision to worry a specific number of minutes at specific times puts your conscious mind in charge of your worry addiction. By putting your conscious mind in charge, you break your unconscious worry patterns without having to spend months or years analyzing them.

As you set up your new schedule, it is best to schedule more time than last week, rather than less time. Otherwise, you may have to struggle too hard against the urge to worry. Increasing time now will make it easier to decrease your time later and then to stop entirely. Decide what feels right to you.

Most people find that three minutes is the absolute maximum for steady worrying. Even if you're the exception, schedule more sessions and less time per session.

If you find that you don't have any idea how often you worry about your Worthless Wonder, you may want to count your worries before you devise your schedule. Do this for at least three days. You can carry a pad of paper and pencil with you and simply make a check mark each time you discover yourself worrying. An easier method is to wear a golfer's stroke counter on your wrist. Each time you worry, press the button. At the end of the day you'll have an exact tally. Then, after three days, answer the questions under New Worry Schedule.

"I WORRY ABOUT WHAT TO COOK FOR MY DINNER PARTY" —NEW WORRY SCHEDULE

1. *When?:* 7:15 A.M. (while showering).
   7:45 A.M. (with my coffee).
   5 P.M. and 5:15 P.M. (while commuting.)
   I want to practice worrying and stopping worrying within the same hour, in order to get in charge of stopping and starting my worry.
2. *How many minutes:* Two minutes per session.

"I WORRY ABOUT NOT SAVING ENOUGH MONEY"—NEW WORRY SCHEDULE

1. *When?:* 7 A.M.
   I don't want to worry at night, because then I have trouble sleeping.
2. *How many minutes:* Three minutes.

"I WORRY BECAUSE MY WAIST IS GETTING FAT AND FLABBY" —NEW WORRY SCHEDULE

1. *When?:* Before each meal and before any other time I eat. If I'm going to worry, that's the best time. Usually I worry after eating, and that's no good at all.
2. *How many minutes?:* One minute each time.

Decide for yourself when you will worry and for how long.

Perhaps you are wondering how you will keep your worry to the tight schedule you have devised? There are several ways of doing it. The simplest is to remind yourself, each time you notice that you are engaged in worthless worrying, that you will do this worrying only at the time you planned. Say to yourself, "Hey, it's ten A.M. and my Worthless Worry time is three P.M. I'll get back to you, old WW, in exactly five hours."

Another way is to imagine your unscheduled worries to be like pests that just creep up. Use an imaginary bug spray to destroy any Worthless Wonders that creep toward you at the wrong time.

Have a substitute mental activity that you can do whenever you are wanting to banish your worry from your mind. Think about your last vacation. Recite to yourself a poem you particularly like or hum a song. Write down a series of grade-school arithmetic problems, and do them.

Remember the old kit bag? During World War I, English soldiers carried them for their personal belongings. In your imagination, get yourself one. By now any existing kit bags would be exceedingly old and probably quite moldy, but so is your Worthless Wonder. Imagine that you are putting your Worthless Wonder into your own old kit bag. Lock the bag and open it only at the times when you have decided to worry. If by chance you find more worthless worries, put them into the bag too. When your worry time comes around, you can have a selection of worries to choose from. Until then,

> **Pack up your troubles in your old kit bag**
> **And smile, smile, smile.**

CHAPTER 27

ACTION NOW, WITH VILLAINS AND HEROES: FIFTH DAY

How have you done with your plans for action? And with your worrying? Did you know that you have only one of four choices:

1. *Stop worrying and take action.* If you have stopped worrying and also begun to implement one of your actions, congratulations. You've used your worry positively, as a trigger for action. You've proved to yourself that you are in charge of your behavior and your own mental processes. Appreciate what you have accomplished. In fact, you may want to give yourself something special to remember what you've done. Perhaps you'd like to take an afternoon off to go to an art exhibit, give yourself a long bubble bath tonight, or get a ticket to a play you've been wanting to see. Do something to mark your achievement as special.

One of the crucial differences between worriers and nonworriers is that nonworriers enjoy the process of problem solving. They look at problems as opportunities to use their ingenuity, rather than as something to worry about. For them that is exciting.

Imagine two people in a new city, each trying to find a particular street address. The worrier fusses over poor directions and unreadable street signs and gets a headache from worrying. The nonworrier enjoys the challenge. When you take action and stop worrying, you can begin to appreciate your own problem-solving abilities.

Each time you turn a worry into a challenge and enjoy that challenge, you are in the ranks of the Ex-Worriers of the World. Again, CONGRATULATIONS.

2. Stop worrying and take no action. If you stopped worrying and decided not to take an action right now, that's fine too. You have learned to separate action from worry and have kept the worrier in your head from making you miserable. Congratulate yourself.

If you want to take action in the future to keep your worry from coming true, go back over your list: who, what, when, where, why, how, and other information. Perhaps you can find a new way of stimulating yourself to do what you can to solve the problem you used to worry about.

No matter what you decide, you have learned that

WORRYING IS IRRELEVANT. WORRYING WILL NOT MAKE YOU TAKE AN ACTION NOR PREVENT YOU FROM TAKING ONE.

3. Take no action and keep worrying. If you decided against taking action and are still worrying, perhaps you should file this worry under Worthless Wonders? Go back to the preceding chapter and figure out a worry schedule for yourself. Or, if you prefer, continue to read this chapter and learn a technique for abolishing the worry villain in your head.

4. Take action and keep worrying. If you are taking an action that is important to you and you are still worrying, you need to tackle the worry villain in your head right now.

Remember the villain in old-fashioned melodramas? He strides onto the stage, twirling his mustache, and over-powers the poor little victim. Villains come in all sorts of shapes and sizes, so invent one who will be your worry-villain. To do this right, you need to turn off your adult self. Be young at heart, as you were when you imagined standing on the podium, bragging to the worriers of the world.

Using your young, creative self, imagine your own personal villain. You can use the mustache twirler, a judge, a bossy big brother or sister, a witch, or any villain you choose. Imagine your villain dressed for the part and give him or her villainous gestures. Then listen to your villain telling you to worry.

The judge: "So you lost two pounds. What's two pounds, anyway? You'll never stick to a diet." The judge waggles a finger and glares. "You'll never keep it up. You'll be back before my court in no time. Wait till some-one tempts you with a chocolate éclair."

The bossy big sister: "You go to college? What a laugh!"

Have you imagined your villain's appearance, ges-tures, and words? Then stand up and practice the role of villain, so that you can feel the part. Exaggerate the ges-tures. Point your finger, shake your fist, scowl horribly. Be a first-class villain, as you say, "Worry!"

When you know that part well, change position and be the poor little victim. You may have thought that the villain is the only hurtful character in your head, but that's not true. Equally hurtful is the victim who listens to the villain. Test it out. Say, "Worry!" one more time. Now be aware that if you tell your villain, "Don't be stupid, I'm not worrying about that," and go on about your business, you'll have no trouble from your villain.

Instead, through the years, you have listened to your

villain. That's what makes you your own worst victim. For your melodrama today, exaggerate your victim part. Let your face and your body show your helpless anger, your sadness, your guilt or fear or shame. Hunch up your shoulders, wring your hands, or look limply pathetic. When you are ready, sound the trumpets!

Here comes the hero! What's your hero like? Perhaps you imagine a good priest or minister, Superman, a warm, kindly, and effective mother, a good cop. Take time to pick out your own hero and dress that hero for the part, as if for a role in a Broadway drama. Imagine your hero walking on stage, seeing the villain and the victim, and saying, "No more! I am taking this victim away from you right now." Or you might prefer a fighting hero, who knocks out the villain or tosses the villain head-over-heels into the brambles.

Superman stands in front of the judge. "Judge, you are prejudiced and corrupt," he snarls. The judge turns pale and begs for mercy. "Take off those robes," Superman demands. "You will never be allowed to be a judge again!" Superman and the victim leave the courtroom in triumph.

A kindly big sister walks in. She puts an arm around the victim and says, "You'll do fine in college." She and the victim walk out together, ignoring the bossy villain.

Be your hero and experience your own real power. Kick your shoes off and stand securely. Bend your knees slightly, and enjoy the firmness of your heels against the floor. You are your own hero! Enjoy the power of your full, easy breathing. Put your hands on your hips, and feel the strength in your shoulders and arms. Let your whole body be strong and powerful. Tell your villain, "I am banishing you." Say to the victim part of you, "From now on, I'm protecting you."

Play all the roles several times. When you are ready, be the victim for the last time. Your hero is beside you. Hug your hero and experience you, the victim, and you, the hero, merging into one powerful person. You can fight back effectively anytime against your internal villain.

In the future, when you hear your villain telling you to worry, experience your power. Say, "I will not victimize myself by listening to worry messages. I choose not to worry." You'll find that, with practice, this becomes easy to do.

CHAPTER 28

RETURNING THE FAMILY WORRIES: SIXTH DAY

In the past five sessions, you've sorted your worries, learned a variety of ways to take conscious charge of them, and begun the process of letting them go.

Today you'll be doing some imaginative personal historical research to learn about your family's worriers. Then you can return your worries to the people who originated them.

Start with family members of your generation. Imagine that you are sitting in the center of a football field with your brothers, sisters, and all the cousins you knew well when you were growing up. How many of them are worriers? Look at them, one at a time, and decide who are the worriers. Give the worriers bright red pennants. Write on each pennant the name of the worry. You can use their childhood worries or the worries they talk about today. Brother Charles may have a pennant that says "School," Cousin Jenny may have one that says "Hair," and someone else may have one that says "Money" or "Jobs." Give the nonworriers yellow pennants.

Notice who waves the yellow and who the red. Are the red pennants primarily for females or primarily for males? In some families the women do the worrying, whereas in others the men are the worriers. Do the older kids in each family tend to be worriers, while the younger ones get to be worry-free? Which color goes to the ones who are considered successful and which to those who are called failures? Who are the heroes and what color pennants do they wave?

In some families the nonworrier is looked down on because that person "didn't care enough about mother" or simply because "that one doesn't take anything seriously." In other families the nonworrier is admired. "Ann is wonderful! Nothing bothers her!" And sometimes it's mixed. Are the worriers labeled more responsible? More intelligent? More caring? More boring? Are the nonworriers labeled more exciting? More fun? Less intelligent? Less caring? What a lot you can learn as you look at the yellow and red pennants around you.

When you are ready, imagine that your parents, aunts, and uncles have arrived to take their places behind your cousins and brothers and sisters. This is the generation who probably taught you to worry. When you have assembled your group, look at each one carefully. Imagine that you can hear them talking about their worries. What worries do they say aloud? What stories do they tell about each other? Give each person a red or yellow pennant and put a name for the worry on each red one. Notice again whether the worriers tend to be male or female, oldest or youngest, happy or sad, heroes or goats? What do you learn from each of them about worrying? Are any of their worries similar to yours?

If you come from a large family, you already have a good size group assembled. Next, bring in the people from your grandparents' generation to sit in the next row. Even though the others may be sitting on the grass, imagine that the grandparents and the great-aunts and great-uncles are on chairs, because that is no doubt how you remember them. These people are the ones who taught your parents to worry. Do you know any famous worry stories about your grandparents?

Jean's aunt told Jean all about how grandfather's worries changed Uncle Henry's career. Uncle Henry was only fourteen years old when the local doctor bought the first automobile in town. Henry was such a natural at mechanics that he was hired to keep the car running. As more people bought automobiles and hired Henry, Henry decided that automobiles would be his life work. He wanted to drop out of high school to set up "repair barns" for cars, but his father worried that it was not a respectable career. "Besides," said his father, "automobiles are tomfoolery and a flash in the pan." He told Henry that everyone would go back to horses just as soon as they got those silly cars out of their systems.

No one knows what Uncle Henry really thought about all this, but in order not to worry his father, Henry finished high school and went to work in his father's bank. He was still working at the bank when almost every family had turned in their horses for cars. He was still working there during the Depression, when all the banks, including theirs, failed. At least Henry had not worried his father.

If you come from a family that doesn't tell stories much, you may have to search your memory hard for any story fragments you may have heard. If your parents or stepparents are living, you might telephone them tonight for a family "worry interview." It goes like this: "Hi," and some pleasant chatter about what is going on in your house and theirs. Then tell them you are doing something new. You are figuring out what your ancestors worried about. Let them know this is just a new game and you'll explain it to them later. You can offer them this book if they are interested. Then begin. "Tell me about my grandparents. When you were a little kid, were they worriers? . . . What especially did they worry about?... Did they tell you any stories about their mothers and fathers worrying?... What about their grandparents?" When you've finished, you may have a lot of fascinating information about the people in your family and how they worried.

Imagine your grandparents on the football field, talking about their worries to you, to your parents, and to their own brothers and sisters. What worries do you hear?

One worrier, listening in fantasy to her grandparents, remembered the time her grandmother caught her going barefoot. Grandmother owned a tiny shoe store in Brooklyn. She told her granddaughter, "If people see you going barefoot, they'll believe that it's all right not to wear shoes in America. Then no one will buy shoes, and we will starve to death."

When you are ready, bring in your great-grandparents and any of their brothers or sisters whom you knew or have heard about. Hand them their pennants. If there are any famous worriers or nonworriers in your family's history, be sure to include them. A famous worrier, for example, is Great-great-uncle George, who never left the house without a knapsack that contained a clean shirt and food so that if he broke a leg, fell in a well, was ambushed by Indians, or simply couldn't find his way back to the house some night, he would be prepared. A famous nonworrier is Great-great uncle Toby, who set out for California and gold without compass, guide, or a care in the world. If there is an Uncle Toby in your family, be sure he is waving a yellow pennant.

Are the worries from your grandparents' and great-grandparents' generations similar to your worries? What are you learning about the way the worries were passed on to you?

Look over all your relatives again to see if there are patterns in their worrying. In some families the righteous worry about faraway have-nots and sinners, and the family is studded with missionaries. In other families they worry about the sinners right at home. In your family did each generation have some misbehaving family member they could worry about?

In some families the primary worry is, "What will the neighbors think?" Other families worry incessantly about money or about health. Did your family worry about things that often did come true or did they make up fantastic worries, like the worry that there would never be enough cars in America to keep young Henry employed?

Now that you have recognized the worries and the worry patterns that you have accepted, are you ready to give them back to the people who taught them to you? Tell them, "I am returning my worries to you." Choose a worry that you share with one of them and invent a statuette about six inches high to represent that worry. You can make it either plain or fancy and of any material you choose. Give your imagination free rein. When you have visualized your statuette, take it to a member of your family.

"Mother, here is a jade heart. You taught me that to love is to worry. I am no longer worrying about the people I love." Imagine that your mother frowns for a moment and then smiles as she hands the heart to her mother, who passes it on to your great-grandmother.

"Hello, Big Brother. You worry about grades. I am giving you a statue of a little boy lugging a great big report card. Just like you, my grades were always fine and still I worried. I'm giving you our worries and I am no longer worrying about being graded."

"Hello, Aunt Frances. You worried all the time about how your hair looked and you explained to me that I had the same awful, stringy hair as you. I am giving you a platinum mirror. I'll do my best with my hair and stop worrying about what I can't change."

"Hello, all of you who are overweight. I see you all, fussing and worrying and not changing your shapes. I'm giving you this miniature scale. I have decided to like myself the way I am."

"Hello, Father. You worry about the future. I'm giving you a crystal ball that says "Disaster" in its center. Whenever I find myself looking into the future with worry, I'll remember the ball and remind myself that I am not going to make up disaster stories about the future."

"Mother and Father and Grandmother Murphy and Grandfather Jones, here is a ceramic poorhouse. It represents all our money worries throughout the years." As you say this, imagine a great-great-grandmother suddenly appearing in the group. She asks, "But didn't our worries keep us out of the poorhouse?" Explain to her that the ability to continue earning a living is important, but the ability to worry is not.

She says, "That isn't what my father taught me."

As you listen to her, you realize that you stopped too soon. Behind every worrier are the parents and grandparents, the aunts and uncles, who taught them to worry. Bring in the rest! Watch the long procession of your ancestors as they file in and take their places on the field and in the stands. They are waving yellow pennants and red pennants. Notice the Old World clothing and be aware that they are talking in languages you've never even heard, including, perhaps, the English of Chaucer, the Spanish of Cervantes, Latin, Hebrew from Solomon's time, Arabic, Oriental languages from thousands of years ago. Filing in last may be the first nomads and the cave people. You'll want to give everyone a set of magic earphones with instant translation so that your family and all your ancestors can understand what's being said.

As you look at this huge group of people, pick out special ancestors who typify your family worry patterns. Have fun with your fantasies.

Perhaps one of your ancestors is the grandfather in *Peter and the Wolf*, by Sergei Prokofiev. Peter did a fantastic job of planning exactly how to catch the wolf safely, caught him, and then got the help of the hunters to stage a triumphal procession as they took the wolf to the zoo. What did Grandfather do? Instead of cheering his active, intelligent, very creative grandson, he "tossed his head discontentedly and asked, 'And if Peter hadn't caught the wolf, what then?' " That grandfather is proud of his red pennant.

Did your ancestors come from countries where there were invasions, mass murders, or plagues? Naturally they looked for magical ways of protecting their loved ones, and perhaps their magic was, "Don't feel too good or something bad will happen!" Imagine them shaking their heads and repeating old stories about how happiness came just before tragedy and how worry might somehow have prevented such tragedies.

They may be telling about the time when the Cossacks rode down on their village and murdered half the people at the wedding dance. Or perhaps your ancestors were wonderfully happy Romans until the Huns came, giving the message, "Don't feel too good or we'll destroy you!" Were your ancestors smiling and eating an extra portion of rice and a plump boiled chicken just when the emperor's samurai swooped down on them? Perhaps one of your ancestors in Puritan New England was caught giggling on the Sabbath and put in the stocks for punishment?

Perhaps one of your ancestors, a hundred generations ago, was a follower of Moses, who worried the whole forty years that they'd never find their way out of the wilderness or, if they did, that whatever they found wouldn't be worth the trek? Bring onto the football field Moses' follower and give him or her a red pennant that says, "Wilderness Worries."

Perhaps your ancestors, the cave people, were celebrating their discovery of the use of fire when the fire got out of hand and burned up all their nice fur blankets? Pick up a magic microphone and call out to all of them, "Human beings do not have to worry."

Imagine the cheers of those who carry the yellow pennants and the perplexed silence of the red-pennant ones. Tell them all that you are returning your worries to them. "Hey, ancestors, a lot of you worried about sin. I'm giving you plastic halos. I never worried about sin. And I never before realized that I was influenced by your worries. But now I know that you taught worrying as preventive medicine against happiness, because you believed that to be happy was to be a sinner. I am no longer using worry to spoil my happiness."

As you look around the football field, you see your great-great-grandmother passing the ceramic poorhouse back to her parents, who pass it back to their parents, who keep passing it back until somehow it disappears as it is handled by ancestors who don't quite understand what a poorhouse is.

Your Aunt Frances is handing her mirror to her grand-mother.

Your father tosses the crystal ball into the air, his mother catches it and tosses it to her father. Watch it glint in the sun as it is tossed further and further back through the generations, until it reaches an old peasant, who says, "My future did turn out miserably, and my son worried that his future would be like mine. That's how the worry started." He keeps the ball.

Big brother's statuette of the boy with the report card goes to a young page from the Middle Ages, who says, "I was so young, and I had to be perfect."

The scales are handed back through the generations, until a great-great grandmother says, "I like my large size," and stamps the scale into the grass.

Invent as many statuettes as you like and give them away. Probably every one of your worries could be returned to some relative, who can pass it back through the generations.

When you have finished giving out individual statu-ettes, ask all of your direct ancestors, from the beginning of time, to stand. Pick up a magic microphone and address the group. "Ladies and gentleman, I thank you." Your progenitors are, truly, a remarkable group. In spite of plagues and wars and famines, every single one of your direct ancestors grew to adulthood and every single one of them was fertile, or you would not exist. Bow to them and thank them again for that gift.

Announce to them all, "I learned to worry, as you did, from those who came before me. Now I am letting my worries go. You didn't need to worry, but you didn't know that. I know that my worries are useless, and I am giving them up." Use the words that fit for you. When you have finished, wave them a kiss, if you like, before you make them disappear.

CHAPTER 29

NOT TO WORRY!

You are now ready to be an ex-worrier. This doesn't mean you'll never worry again. When you receive distressing news, you may worry as you decide what you can do. When you have to make choices without a guarantee of the outcome, you may worry briefly. But now you can be free of repetitive, addictive worrying. If you should at some time fall back into these worry patterns, you have other options. You can look for solutions and praise yourself for taking action. You can postpone your worries to specific times of the day. You can substitute other thoughts and fantasies for your worries. You can change the endings so that your worries amuse you rather than distress you. You can recognize when your worries are beyond your power to solve and let them go. You can return your worries to your ancestors.

This is a review session. Before reading it, give yourself at least a week to practice what you've learned so far.

PIDDLING WORRIES

What have you done with your piddling worry? Did you stop worrying about it when you realized that it really was piddling? Some people do. If you did, that's wonderful! Did you stop worrying after turning it into a silly story with an absurd ending? Or did you use another method to give up your worry? Whatever your method, when you stop a worry, you prove to yourself that you are in charge. That is the first and most important step in breaking free from a worry addiction. Hurrah for you!

Do you have any other piddling worries lurking somewhere in the back of your mind? If not, don't try to dredge one up. But if you do, tell yourself, "Worries about insignificant matters are beneath my dignity. I've outgrown these worries." Anytime you think of one of them again, do it with interest rather than worry. "Oh, how interesting. I'm all of a sudden about to worry that something will go wrong on my trip to the West Coast. I suppose I am having a flashback to my worry years." Just as dry alcoholics dream they are drinking, ex-worriers find themselves remembering old worries. Sometimes you may even become aware that you are watching a worry movie in your mind. If you get lost while driving, you may suddenly see an old "lost forever in the big city" drama haunting you until you remember that you know how to turn off your internal projector. Then, if necessary, you'll ask directions.

If you have not yet given up your piddling worry, there may be a simple explanation. Perhaps you are having difficulty with the concept that your worry could be piddling. Even though you classified it that way, it still feels important to you. That is probably because your worry was important in the past. A dinner-party worry is earth-shaking to the child who watches mother scrub every corner of the house, shine the silver, desperately make every closet perfect, and then in exhaustion begin to cook. That child can grow into an adult who doesn't classify the fantasized ruin of a party as trivial.

If you are still worrying about something piddling, you might enjoy exaggerating its importance. "I don't care if the entire world bans worry, I will uphold my right to worry about my dinner parties. And on my tombstone will be engraved, 'She cared enough to worry about the pot roast she served her friends.' " After you've taken that side, you may be more ready to drop your worry. Or you may enjoy your exaggeration and decide to practice turning your piddling worries into full-blown soap operas as you fight for your right to maintain them.

MIDDLE-SIZE AND SIGNIFICANT WORRIES

How have you done with your middle-size and significant worries? If you have stopped worrying about them, congratulations! You have given yourself a tremendous gift. You are recovering from your addiction, and that is wonderful for you.

Worry really is useless. Looking for options is what counts, and you can do that without worrying.

Have you other middle-size or significant worries? If so, sort them into Creative Fiction, Beyond My Skill, Worthless Wonders, and Action Now. With practice you'll be able to recognize the Action Now worries almost as soon as you think of them and then decide what you will do to keep them from coming true. You'll also recognize more and more quickly which of your worries are beyond your skill to solve.

Have you discovered the pleasure and sheer relief of no longer worrying? Perhaps after giving a middle-size or significant worry to your ancestors, you woke the next morning without your habitual worries and heard the birds singing and were aware that you had not listened to them in a long time. That is a gift from a worry-free mind. When you experience this freedom, you'll know how much you had deprived yourself. You'll feel new and open. It's a feeling similar to the way you felt in childhood, the morning you woke feverless and well after an illness. Worry is a kind of illness.

CREATIVE FICTION

Did you enjoy changing your Creative Fiction worries into silly stories? Besides being a fun way to stop worrying, writing these stories also helps you practice using the right hemisphere of your brain. As you imagine impossible endings or characters that never existed, you stimulate your ability to be intuitive and inventive. This is called right-brain activity, as contrasted with left-brain, practical thinking, which is based on facts. Want some more right-brain fun with worries?

- Keep turning them into absurd stories.
- Use magic guns or bows and arrows to shoot your worries away.
- Use waterfalls and fast streams to carry them away.
- Melt them or burn them or send them into orbit.
- Invent dragons to breathe fire and burn them up.
- Turn your worry into a big balloon and prick it.
- Wrap your worry carefully and send it to the Dead Letter Office.
- Put your worry onto a film and either speed up or slow down the action. As you do this, hear the voices becoming scratchy-high, like chipmunks', or slow and heavy. Watch the movie characters race madly or barely move.

Invent a new, silly gimmick for each new worry.

BEYOND MY SKILL

If you have stopped worrying about problems that are beyond your skill to solve, congratulations!

If you still have some difficulty with them, use the Serenity Prayer: "God grant me the serenity to accept the things I cannot change, the courage to change the things I can, and the wisdom to know the difference." If one of your worries is beyond your skill to change, grant yourself the wisdom to know this. Permit yourself serenity with your wisdom. Grant yourself the peace that comes from letting these worries go. Alcoholics call this "turning it over" to a higher power. A higher power is whoever or whatever you believe it to be. For you, your higher power may be God or the spiritual oneness of humanity or even the serene part of yourself.

Pause long enough to memorize the Serenity Prayer and give yourself permission to use it whenever you worry yourself about something that is beyond your skill to solve.

Instead of worrying, take yourself in your imagination to a special, tranquil place. You are walking through an old orchard of big, heavy apple trees, covered with white blossoms. Above, the sky is very blue and the clouds are as fluffy and white as the blossoms. In the middle of the orchard you find your very own apple tree. You put one foot on the lowest branch, grab a higher one, and swing yourself up. Feel the good roughness of the bark against your hands. Now let yourself climb up three more branches, and there, hidden from the ground by the myriad blossoms, is your secret seat. It's a piece of wood nailed across two branches, and it's perfectly safe for sitting. Let yourself sit on your secret seat. You are hidden from the world. All you can see, on all sides, are branches and blossoms, and you know this is your fairyland.

Do you prefer a roof hideaway? Climb the stairs to the top floor of a building and push open the door. The roof is flat, with lots of chimneys sticking out of it. Some are tiny with little tin caps on them, and some are big and tall. You pretend they are all friendly soldiers guarding you. Walk to the biggest chimney and sit in its shade, with your back leaning against its yellowish brick. From there you can see taller buildings and, far away, a tiny hint of sea. The breeze blows on your face and the sun warms you.

Pick a happy place, real or imaginary, to go when you find yourself worrying about problems that are Beyond My Skill.

WORTHLESS WONDER

How did you do? Did you leave yourself sufficient time for your worry? Perhaps three times a day was right for you, but you prefer worrying only one minute instead of five minutes per worry session? Perhaps you need more sessions? Fewer sessions? Did you sometimes forget to worry? Now may be a good time to revise your schedule for next week. Don't push yourself to give up your schedule. You'll know when you are ready.

ACTION NOW

CONGRATULATE YOURSELF FOR THE CHANGES YOU HAVE MADE AND THE ACTIONS YOU HAVE TAKEN! Find a way of rewarding yourself. Giving yourself small, loving, congratulatory gifts is a splendid way of encouraging yourself to keep growing and making changes in your life.

SUMMARY

Here is a quick formula for sorting your worries.

1. Is my worry based on reality or fantasy? (If fantasy, it is Creative Fiction.)
2. Is there anything I can do to prevent it from coming true? (If not, it is Beyond My Skill.)
3. If there is something I can do, do I choose to do it? (If not, it is a Worthless Wonder.)
4. Whether or not I choose to do what I can to prevent my worry from coming true, I WILL STOP WORRYING NOW.

As you've noticed, some antiworry techniques work better with some worries than with others. Fantasy and imagery are for Creative Fiction worries, serenity and "turning it over" are for worries that are Beyond My Skill, behavior modification tools are for Worthless Wonders, and problem solving is the appropriate method to deal with worries that you classify as Action Now. However, this is not always true. Sometimes the personality of the worrier counts more than anything else.

If you are a logical person who does not like fantasy, use the behavior modification techniques. Set specific worry times. Use a stroke counter. Make a worry chart, using a line or a bar graph on which you tabulate worries. If you want a fancy chart, use a different color ink for each category of worry. That way you can keep track of which types of worries you are dropping and which ones you are keeping. You can clock when you start and stop each worry in order to chart the amounts of time you spend worrying. As you do this, you'll become less and less addicted to your worries.

Use positive reinforcement by praising every move you make toward ending your worries while ignoring any backsliding. In fact, you can logically decide that you have cured yourself of your worry addiction as soon as you have learned to start and stop worries on schedule.

To expand your repertoire, you may enjoy the Serenity Prayer, which is also logical.

You can trace the origin of each of your worries and even draw up a Family Worry Tree, going back as many generations as you can.

If you are spiritual rather than logical in your approach to life, you probably prefer turning your worries over to a higher power. You can use that technique for all worries. You only need your logical mind for deciding whether to take action to keep a worry from becoming a reality. You may also use meditation, sensory-awareness experiences, and fantasy trips as substitutes for worry.

If you love fantasy and enjoy inventing it, use fantasy and nonsense to battle all your worries. You can even use your right-brain creativity when you are looking for solutions to the worries you label Action Now. The villains-and-heroes drama is especially fine for you. You can also enjoy inventing new scenes in which you return your worries to your ancestors. You might even fantasize collaborating with them in setting up a huge worry-burial, complete with eulogies and music brought in by all the generations.

Whether you prefer logic, a spiritual approach, or fantasy, keep the villains out of your head and practice being your own hero.

No technique is better than another. You decide which you prefer, and that will be the best method for you. Use it until you can declare yourself an Ex-Worrier of the World.

PART IV

CHAPTER 30

HOW TO LIVE IN A WORLD OF WORRIERS AND NOT GO CRAZY

Now that you are an ex-worrier, you may have joined the ranks of all the people who would like to know how to associate with worriers and not go crazy. The worriers in your life may be your boss, your best employee, your favorite golf partner, your parents, your children, or your lover.

Worriers are everywhere. And they are difficult people. They will admit that. Why do people put up with them? If you are an ex-worrier, you put up with worriers in the past because, being one, you didn't know better. Also, you may have associated with worriers for the same reason that heavy drinkers associate with alcoholics, to prove that, by comparison, "There's nothing wrong with me." If you've never been a worrier, the reasons may be more complicated. Growing up with worriers, you may have become used to them or dependent on them to do your worrying for you.

Ex-worrier or nonworrier, you also put up with the worriers in your life because you respect them or like them or love them.

Your worrying boss is fine in every other way. Your worrying employee is the only one who gets to work early and sticks with a problem until it's solved.

Your worrying father raised you and cares about you. Your worrying auntie sends you five dollars every Christmas and introduced you to art museums when you were a child.

Your happy, bright, caring, sexy partner is the love of your life.

Worriers are nice people, and many of them are also wonderful. If they know the art of dramatic worrying, even their worries may be entertaining at times.

However much you may care about or love your worriers, you still need to protect yourself from them. Otherwise, you'll find yourself becoming a co-dependent. Co-dependents of worriers are like co-dependents of alcoholics, in that they let the behavior of the other person run, and sometimes ruin, their lives. Co-dependents may be reassurers, rebels, caretakers, or slaves. They may be seduced into becoming worry addicts too. They may withdraw from family life. Whatever their role, it is not autonomous. Their behavior is in reaction to the worry addicts in their lives, and that is why they are co-dependent.

Co-dependents who are rebels seem compelled to give the worrier "something to worry about." They come home late, mess up the checking account, or refuse to see physicians when they are obviously ill. Jean's nephew, a very intelligent, law-abiding young man, mentioned at a family gathering, "Since I speak Spanish and can sail, I could probably get a job drug running." The worriers had a field day, not even realizing that he was teasing them. Other rebels may not be teasing when they threaten to make a worrier's worst worries come true.

The reassurers attempt to mitigate the curse of the worries. "Well, even if she drops out of college, she'll go back someday. You'll find out that everything will work out for the best." "I'm sure you don't have to worry about the acid rain. One of these days they'll discover a way to save the trees." These Pollyannas make true worriers climb the walls! There is nothing more aggravating to a worrier than to have little rays of sunshine interspersed into their most dramatic worry tales. The reassurer ends up scorned and even vilified. "How can you be so naive!" "You are totally incapable of understanding the problem!"

To keep from being inundated by the worries around them, other reassurers become dried-out adults who stick obsessively to facts. If the worrier says, "I am so worried about your job," the co-dependent brings out whole statistical tables proving there is no cause for worry. This never satisfies the worrier, so the co-dependent rushes out to seek more facts in the frantic belief that someday the perfect fact will stop all worries. The only relevant fact is: facts have never cured a worry addiction.

A real worrier will win against any logical argument you may muster. You can prove to a worrier that the chances are 15 million to one that a worry won't come true, and the worrier will focus on that one chance. Although this type of reasoning is absurd, it is not unusual. The odds against winning the jackpot in the California lottery have been 15 million to one, and yet millions of Californians throw their money into it every week. Why should you expect worry addicts to be more rational than millions of amateur gamblers?

Some co-dependents function as slaves, rushing to do the bidding of the worrier. If the worrier is concerned about money, the co-dependent writes a check. If a worrying mother believes that one of her grown children is not functioning well at home or at work, the co-dependent telephones this person to say, "You must stop what you are doing, because your mother is sick with worry about you." The co-dependent is in the dreadful position of being dis-

liked by all. The worrier believes that the co-dependent isn't
trying hard enough, while the others are furious at the at-
tempted manipulations.

Some co-dependents remain sad or angry, waiting for
their worriers to change. They consider the worries to be
personal affronts rather than evidence of addiction and say
sadly, "You don't trust me," or angrily, "When are you going
to stop worrying about me and let me live my own life!"

Some co-dependents ultimately withdraw from their
worriers, finding themselves second jobs or second lovers.
Some learn to sit at work or at home and not hear anything
at all.

What can you do to escape co-dependency?

Most important, recognize that you may ask worriers to
change, but you cannot make them do it. Like alcoholics,
some do change and some do not, and their worrying is
never under your control. It's true that sometimes a worrier
will stop telling you worries, and you'll think you've won.
You may even feel like an absolute monarch of absolutely
everything. But you aren't, as you'll discover the next time
the person tells you a worry. There is no better way to
experience impotence than to try to force a worrier to stop
worrying. Worrying is a psychological addiction, and not
everyone is ready to break free.

Co-dependents are stuck because they think freedom
lies in changing the worrier. Each move they make, each
emotion they feel, is based on hopes and wishes that the
worrier will quit worrying. What they do not realize is that
their own recovery can only occur when they free themselves from psychological bondage. That day will occur
when the co-dependents take charge of their own lives instead of blaming the worrier for their thoughts, feelings,
and actions. When co-dependents recognize that they are
powerless to change another person but are capable of
changing themselves, co-dependency is over.

After you have accepted the fact that you are not in charge

of the worrier's brain, what can you do to make life with worriers easier to bear?

First, monitor yourself so that you don't set up worries. Never ask a hypochondriac, "How are you?" Don't confide your own upsets or problems unless absolutely necessary. Announce your own life changes optimistically and not until you are psychologically ready to withstand the worries you may hear in return. When visiting a worrier, talk about benign aspects of the past or stay rigidly in the present. Find the worriers' "worry-free zones." If your worrier likes discussing literature, you can spend pleasant, worry-free hours on this subject.

Set up ground rules. You have a right to say, "I have decided I won't listen to worries." Then, when the worrier telephones to present a worry, you can ask, "What good happened today?"

If the worrier persists, ask, "Otherwise, how are you?"

If the worrier still persists, say, "Good-bye."

This is an extreme method, and perhaps you would prefer to interject, "As I mentioned to you earlier, I don't listen to worries," between "Otherwise, how are you?" and "Good-bye."

Before a visit to a worrier's home, do the same. "I've decided that while I'm visiting you, Dad, I'm not going to listen to worries. I love you very much and when you talk about your worries, I don't enjoy it. In fact, I get upset. So I've made a rule for myself. From now on, whenever anybody talks about worries, I'm going for a walk or taking a drive instead of listening." It's important to follow through. When he starts in on his worries, tell him, "I'm going for a walk to get my head clear of worries. I'll be back in ten minutes." Stay loving and stay firm.

Don't get caught up in the worries. No matter how seductive the worry, don't let yourself begin to worry with the worrier. Remind yourself that worries are fiction and that you are not going to let your own emotional life be influenced by other people's fiction. If you are going to suffer from worries, at least let them be your own.

There are dozens of ways to stay out of the worry traps. One of your best defenses is to enjoy thinking up novel responses to worries. You might begin by being nurturing and supportive. "You are a good person, and I am sorry you worry so much. I wish you wouldn't torture yourself that way." "Are you tired? Sometimes, when you are tired, you add to your troubles by worrying. We could just sit quietly and I'll give you a back rub."

Another time you might choose to be critical. "Worrying is a bore!" "Stop telling me your worries about my son. Your worries suggest he can't handle his own affairs, and I won't listen to you put him down."

Just for fun, be a wacky nurturer. A worrier with a sense of humor might respond with laughter. "If we sold the house and became bagpeople, we wouldn't have to worry about the roof and the plumbing." Or, "I could do your worrying for you on Sundays, to give you a day of rest."

Use love to shut off worries: "I love you." Use compliments: "Your dress brings out the beautiful hazel in your eyes," or "In that shirt you look so sexy."

Use activities: "Come on, let's go make cookies," or "How about a quick swim in the pool?"

If you are tempted to introduce facts to rebut a worry, remember that facts don't help, but irrelevant facts might distract you both: "Did you notice in the paper that you can now book tours that land in Antarctica? If I went on a tour like that, I wonder if I could find out how penguins sleep without freezing?" Or, "I once read that ninety-two percent of the people who have head colds were hit on the head at least once in their childhood. Now that doesn't necessarily imply a connection, but I find it a most interesting thought."

Your own humor can keep you free, whether you say it aloud or merely think it.

Sweetly: "Instead of worrying about the car, let's worry about something more fun, like arson and murder."

Angrily: "Isn't it awful that this world is created the way it is, so that poor people like us have to worry, while our president just goes off and has a good time?"

Sadly: "Oh, that would be tragic if it came true. I know a family who is in even sadder trouble. Let me tell you all about them."

Fearfully: "It's probably one hundred percent worse than you can even imagine!"

Resignedly, between sighs: "Oh, I do worry about that. I also worry about the dolphins and the whales, and did you notice that your neighbor's lawn isn't doing well this year?"

Learn to search for one-liners when you are stuck listening to a worrier, but only use them with worriers who like to laugh with you.

> Worrier: "I'm so worried about Dan. He doesn't seem happy in his work."
> Response: "That's because he's underqualified for any job anywhere."

> Worrier: "You don't seem to be saving money."
> Response: "That's true. And I also have pimples."

> Worrier: "I worry about asking for a raise."
> Response: "Me, too. If they paid us what we're worth, we'd both starve."

> Worrier: "I worry what your boss will think of you, going to work in that shirt."
> Response: "If I were hired for my wardrobe, I'd be selling cotton candy for Ringling Brothers."

> Worrier: "Whenever my house isn't clean enough, I worry that someone will drop by for a visit."
> Response: "That's easy. Pull the drapes and hide under the bed."

Worrying Boss: "What if this doesn't pan out?"
Response: "I can shoot you or me. Which will
it be?"

Practice inventing one-liners to keep yourself interested, creative, and nonworrying. Don't say them aloud
except to the very special worriers who like them.

Sometimes a spontaneous one-liner may bring results.
Nick's mother worried incessantly about his health. Whenever the boy had a cold, she'd fuss that he was probably
coming down with pneumonia. One day, when he was
eleven years old, he really was sick. His throat ached and
he felt awful. He raced into the house and yelled hoarsely,
"Mama, take me to the hospital right now. I have pneumonia." She said, "No, you don't!" He was astonished and
also thrilled, knowing he'd found a magic formula for
dealing with his mother. From then on, instead of arguing
that he was well, he agreed with her worries and exag-
gerated them. If she said he was ill, he'd demand an
ambulance. She stopped worrying about his health and
instead concentrated her worries on his sister and father.

Whatever technique you use to keep yourself free of
co-dependency, it is important that you understand the
worriers in your life. It isn't fun to worry. Some ex-
worriers have called worrying "constant dreariness" and
"a pestilence in my brain." Many worriers don't know
there is any other way to be, because they have listened
to a litany of worry since they were babies. Worrying
seems natural and inevitable to them. It honestly doesn't
occur to them that they could give themselves happy
thoughts instead.

Although you can't make a worrier change, you can
offer alternatives. Instead of saying, "You shouldn't
worry," share your own happy thoughts. Give examples
of the fun you have working out solutions to problems.
Keep yourself focused on what you have rather than on
what you lack. When your worrier worries, you can talk

about the good times you expect in the future. If you are willing, give examples of some of your favorite fantasies.

Appreciate aloud any worry-free conversation the two of you have. "This talk has been so much fun." Or, "Thanks for telling me about that article on gardening. I enjoyed listening to you." Or, "You are so much fun. I love the way you are giggling."

If your worrier begins to make changes, going for an evening or even a few days without worrying, prove to both of you that life without worry is beautiful. Be loving and exciting. Dramatic worry stories of gloom and doom may be more interesting than a boring life, so show your lover that life doesn't have to be boring. Then, when your lover moves back into worries, stand off a bit if you like, but don't be sad or angry. Shrug your shoulders, find your own interests, and plan for fun during the next worry-free times. That way you can begin to prove to both of you that worries, even those done by experts, are a poor substitute for the wonderful life you can have together.

There are times when life is not wonderful. With any person, recognize the difference between repetitive worrying and genuine grief. While you appreciate a worrier's joy, it is important to remember that he or she may also want to share unhappiness. When your office partner tells you, "Ray and I are breaking up and I am miserable," he needs your empathic listening. That is very different from the obsessive worry, "What if something happens someday and Ray and I break up?"

When your spouse tells you that your child is having school difficulties, allow yourself to listen to both your spouse and your child and to help them both look for solutions to the problem.

When facing surgery, people need to tell their worries rather than pretend everything is going to be just fine.

Your father's worries may be an indication that he is ill or depressed and needs professional help.

When you successfully resist the co-dependent role, you'll find it much easier to know when the worrier is genuinely distressed rather than obsessively worrying. If in doubt, ask the worrier.

If you live with a worrier, be good to yourself. Have activities that divert you from full-time listening, such as a stamp collection, crossword puzzles, or music. Worriers are draining, and you have a right not to be drained. Set up worry-free activities for the two of you. And set up worry-free activities just for you. You need time away from the worrier. Get positive, nonworrying friends in your life. If your spouse is a worrier, it is crazy to pick worriers for golf partners.

If you have children, give them protection. Children need to know that they did not cause their parents or grandparents to be worriers. Be sure they understand that these adults worried before the children were even born. Tell them that a worrier is always on the prowl for subject matter and that children, by their very existence, are used as subject matter. It is never the child's fault! They are not guilty and they are not responsible for grown-ups' problems. Help them in every way you can, so that they won't grow up to be either worriers or co-dependents.

Teach them to look critically at worries. What are the facts? What are the false premises? The fallacies? As soon as they are old enough to know the difference between past and present, real and unreal, help them to recognize that worries are unreal because they are in the domain of the future. Teach them the fun of problem solving.

Above all, be a nonworrying, supportive role model in their lives. Teach your children, by example, to look into the future with excitement rather than with anxiety.

INDEX